Schoolyear Activities Planner

to accompany

Teaching Language Arts, Fourth Edition, by Carole Cox

■ ■

Carole Cox

California State University, Long Beach

Allyn and Bacon

Boston   London   Toronto   Sydney   Tokyo   Singapore

Senior Editor: Aurora Martinez
Editorial Assistant: Beth Slater
Editorial-Production Administrator: Beth Houston
Editorial-Production Service: Susan Freese, Communicáto, Ltd.
Text Design/Electronic Composition: Denise Hoffman
Composition Buyer: Linda Cox
Manufacturing Buyer: Julie McNeill
Cover Administrator: Linda Knowles

ISBN 0–205–35389–4

Schoolyear Activities Planner

This month-by-month planner provides teaching ideas and activities that reflect the theory, research, and best practices in the text, *Teaching Language Arts*. You can use these ideas and activities in your field experiences or your first year of teaching. I have used a lot of them, as have many of the students in my language arts methods courses and many of the teachers I have written about in the book.

Each month in the planner is divided into four sections:

1. *Language and Literacy Experiences:* This section lists ideas for teaching the language arts that reflect the philosophical foundations of the text. Some are thematic and might be used only at certain times of year, but others could be part of your regular daily program, such as sharing and journal writing.
2. *Lesson Plans:* Two lesson plans relate to the theme of the month. The grade level and purpose of each lesson is noted, followed by the teaching sequence for the lesson and ideas for extending activities for other language arts and cross-curricular lessons.
3. *Children's Books and Films:* Quality books and films related to the theme of the month are listed. Many of the books are excellent for reading aloud, discussing in literature circles, and writing responses.
4. *Websites:* Find out more about each month's theme by visiting the websites listed and described.

This month-by-month planner for the schoolyear is based on themes that are universal, can be used across the grades, and have potential for "ripple effects" across the curriculum:

September: Me and My Family
October: Fall
November: We're All Pilgrims
December: Celebrations
January: Winter

February: Black History Month
March: Women's History Month
April: Spring
May: Ecology
June: The Future

To help you find good-quality children's literature for use in teaching these themes, consult the lists of Newbery and Caldecott Medal–winning and honor books at the end of this planner. Both awards are given annually by the Association for Library Service to Children of the American Library Association.

I'd love to know what happens when you try these ideas and to hear your suggestions for revisions and additions. Please write to me at this address:

Carole Cox
College of Education
California State University–Long Beach
Long Beach, CA 90840
E-mail: cacox@csulb.edu.

Writing about Others

■ *Interviews:* Students develop questions in class to ask each other or family members, school teachers or staff, or community helpers.

■ *Recording Interviews:* During the interviews, students take notes or audio- or videotape them.

■ *Sharing Interviews:* Students write biographies or edit and show the videotaped interviews.

Lesson Plan: *I Like Me!*

Level: Primary to middle grades

Purpose: Listen to, enjoy, and respond to literature of self-esteem.

Teaching Sequence:

1. Read aloud the book *I Like Me!* (Carlson, 1988), about a "pretty pink pig" with good self-esteem who tells all the things she likes about herself and is her own best friend.
2. Use aesthetic, open-ended questions and prompts to discuss the book:
   - "What did you think of the book?"
   - "What was your favorite part?"
   - "What are some of the things you like about yourself?"
3. Create a "word wall" on chartpaper by writing down the children's ideas. Use the heading "WHAT I LIKE ABOUT ME!"
4. Using the word wall as a model, children do a cluster of ideas of what they like about themselves, draw pictures to illustrate them, and write captions. Emerging writers can write their names and then give dictation to the teacher to label or write captions on their pictures.

Extending Activities:

1. Read and discuss *ABC, I Like Me!* (Carlson, 1997), and encourage children to share more things they like about themselves.
2. Create an ABC "word wall" of the words children use to describe what they like about themselves. To categorize the words alphabetically, create a chart like this on a large piece of chartpaper:

ABC, I Like Me!

A	B	C	D	E	F	G	H
I	J	K	L	M	N	O	P
Q	R	S	T	U	V	W	XYZ

Write the words children give you under the appropriate letter headings (e.g., *smile* goes under *S*). You can also create a "word wall" using Post-its or notecards, which you can post and arrange in a variety of ways.

3. Have each child pick a letter, write a sentence to go with it, and illustrate it.
4. Create a class *ABC, I Like Me!* book by compiling children's writing and drawings.
5. Read *Something Special* (McPhail, 1988), *Amazing Grace* (Hoffman, 1991), *The Day of Ahmed's Secret* (Heide & Gilliand, 1990), or *Cleversticks* (Ashley, 1992).

Lesson Plan: *Biopoems*

Level: Middle elementary through middle school grades

Purpose: Write autobiographical poetry using descriptive words.

Teaching Sequence:

1. Read and discuss autobiographical poetry, such as *Something on My Mind* (Grimes, 1978) and *A Fire in My Hands* (Soto, 1990).
2. Make a T-chart of good descriptive words. On the left side, jot down the words used in the poems. On the right side, jot down words the students could use to describe themselves.
3. Have each student make his or her own list of words that describe him or her. Have students use the following frame to write their own biopoems:

BIOPOEM

First name

Four words that tell about you

Child of

Lover of (3 things)

Who feels (3 things)

Who needs (3 things)

Who would like to see (3 things)

Resident of

Last name

Extending Activities:

1. Read more autobiographical poetry: *Cool Salsa: Bilingual Poems on Growing Up Latino in the United States* (Carlson, 1994) and *In Daddy's Arms I Am Tall: African Americans Celebrating Fathers* (Steptoe, 1997).
2. Ask children to illustrate their biopoems with drawings or perhaps scanned photographs, which can be merged with the text of the poem on computer.
3. Collect the students' biopoems in a class book, on a bulletin board, or as a HyperStudio project. (See Chapter 13 in the text for more on HyperStudio projects.)

Children's Books

Angelou, M. (1993). *Life doesn't frighten me.* New York: Stewart, Tabori, and Chang.

Ashley, B. (1992). *Cleversticks.* New York: Crown.

Brown, M. W. (1999). *Another important book.* New York: HarperCollins.

Carlson, L. M. (Ed.). (1994). *Cool salsa: Bilingual poems on growing up Latino in the United States.* New York: Holt.

Carlson, N. (1988). *I like me.* New York: Viking.

Carlson, N. (1997). *ABC, I Like Me!* New York: Viking.

Cisneros, S. (1994). *Hairs/Politos.* New York: Knopf.

Danziger, P. (1999). *I, Amber Brown.* New York: Putnam.

Frasier, D. (1991). *On the day you were born.* New York: Harcourt Brace Jovanovich.

Friedman, I. (1984). *How my parents learned to eat.* Boston: Houghton Mifflin.

Grimes, N. (1978). *Something on my mind.* New York: Dial.

Hausherr, R. (1997). *Celebrating families.* New York: Scholastic.

Heide, F., & Gilliand, J. (1990). *The day of Ahmed's secret.* New York: Lothrop, Lee & Shepard.

Hoberman, M. A. (1991). *Fathers, mothers, sisters, brothers: A collection of family poems.* New York: Penguin.

Hoffman, M. (1991). *Amazing Grace.* New York: Dial.

Lomas Garza, C. (1990). *Family pictures: Cuadros de familia.* New York: Children's Book Press.
McPhail, D. (1988). *Something special.* Boston: Little, Brown.
Rylant, C. (1985). *The relatives came.* New York: Bradbury Books.
Soto, G. (1990). *A fire in my hands.* New York: Scholastic
Soto, G. (1997). *Snapshots from the wedding.* New York: Putnam.
Steptoe, J. (1997). *In Daddy's arms I am tall: African Americans celebrating fathers.* New York: Lee & Low.

Websites
Go to the Official Gary Soto website: **www.garysoto.com.**
Find links to exploring family history on the Genealogy Home Page: **www.genhomepage.com.**

 **Fall**

Language and Literacy Experiences

Drawing and Writing Observations
■ *Nature:* Students record weather observations in a community journal kept by a classroom window; take a nature walk and record observations on paper on lap boards outside; bring samples of fallen leaves or dried plants to class and draw and write about them.

Pattern and Poetry Reading and Writing
■ *Poetry Collections:* The teacher reads aloud poetry collections and students write Halloween poems. Suggested books include *It's Halloween* (Prelutsky, 1977), *Hey-How for Halloween* (Hopkins, 1974), and *Halloween Poems* (Livingston, 1989). Or the teacher may read *The Thirteen Days of Halloween* (Greene, 1990) and have everyone write a class version.

■ *Hands-On Experiences:* Children make crayon rubbings of fall leaves; create a "word wall" about leaves changing color, texture, and shape; write diamante patterns (see Chapter 11) about leaves; carve pumpkins; create a "word wall" of describing words; write triante patterns (see Lesson Plan).

Arts and Crafts
■ *Drawing and Painting:* Through the month of October, students draw or paint trees in the schoolyard that change color once a week and then write about the changes. Students can also examine a piece of popcorn under a microscope; draw it; and write describing words on it to create a concrete poem (see Chapter 10).

■ *Masks:* Children create masks using manila folders, paper plates, or construction paper (see Chapter 6). See *Traditions around the World: Masks* (Earl & Sensier, 1995) and *Pablo Remembers: The Fiesta of the Day of the Dead* (Ancona, 1993).

Drama
■ *Story Dramatization:* Students dramatize a story such as *Where the Wild Things Are* (Sendak, 1963), *Clyde Monster* (Crowe, 1964), *There's a Nightmare in my Closet* (Mayer, 1968), or *Esteban and the Ghost* (Hancock, 1983).

■ *Shakespeare:* Do the witches scene from *Macbeth* (see Chapter 6). See *Shakespeare & Macbeth: The Story behind the Play* (Ross, 1994).

Lesson Plan: *Popcorn*

Level: All grades

Purpose: Build skills in experienced-based talking, writing, and concept and vocabulary development.

Teaching Sequence:

1. Pop popcorn and pass it out on paper napkins for children to eat. Ask them for words that describe the sight and touch of popcorn. Record the words on chartpaper under these headings:

      Smell   Touch   Sight   Sound   Is like/reminds me of

2. Ask the children if popcorn reminds them of anything (e.g., going to the movies, a family story), and record their ideas on a "word wall."

3. Write a class triante using words from the word wall on chartpaper:

      Line 1: One-word   Title
      Line 2: Two words   Smell
      Line 3: Three words   Touch
      Line 4: Four words   Sight
      Line 5: Five words   Sound

4. Writing options: Emerging writers can draw pictures and label them, using describing words from the word wall or giving dictation to the teacher or aide. Older students can write their own triantes using the class triante as a pattern and words from the word wall. Students can also write popcorn stories: what popcorn reminds them of, family experience, and so on.

5. Read *The Popcorn Book* (de Paola, 1978).

Extending Activities:

1. Do some of the things suggested by *The Popcorn Book*: Compare the numbers of kernels that pop after the popcorn has been kept in the refrigerator in an airtight container versus exposed to the air; record observations. Cook popcorn using the two different recipes in the back of the book.

2. Read and write *pourquoi* tales like the Native American one in *The Popcorn Book*: Africa, *Why Mosquitoes Buzz in People's Ears* (Aardema, 1985); Brazil, *Feathers Like a Rainbow: An Amazon Indian Tale* (Flora, 1989); Cambodia, *Judge Rabbit and the Tree Spirit: A Folktale from Cambodia* (Wall, 1991).

3. Make collages by gluing popcorn on black construction paper, and write about the images.

4. Grow popcorn seeds; soak them overnight and plant in a plastic cup. Observe and measure plant growth, and record changes in a journal.

5. Read *Popcorn* (Selsam, 1976) or *Corn Is Maize* (Aliki, 1988).

6. Watch and discuss the film *ZEA* (1982). (See Chapter 6 in the text on film study.)

Lesson Plan: *Pumpkins*

Level: Primary to middle grades

Purpose: Build skills in experience-based talking, writing, and concept and vocabulary development.

Teaching Sequence:
1. Carve a large pumpkin into a jack-o-lantern, and let children touch the rind and the seeds. Put a lighted candle inside the jack-o-lantern, and turn off the lights to let it come to life.
2. Ask the children for words that describe carving the pumpkin into a jack-o-lantern, and use them to create a cluster.
3. As a class, use the words from the cluster to write a poem following the cinquain pattern (see Chapter 4), as shown here:

> **Cinquain**
> Line 1: Title
> Line 2: Description
> Line 3: Action
> Line 4: Feeling
> Line 5: Refers to title

4. Use any of these writing options, depending on the grade level of your students:
   - Have emerging writers draw pictures of a pumpkin and label them, either writing words from the cluster by themselves or giving dictation to the teacher or the aide and having him or her write the labels.
   - Older students can use the words from the cluster and the class cinquain to write their own cinquains.
   - Have students use other poem patterns, such as concrete poetry (see Chapter 10) in the shape of a pumpkin or jack-o-lantern for younger students or for older students, diamante (see Chapter 11), going from a pumpkin to a jack-o-lantern.

Extending Activities:
1. Ask individual children or small groups of children to draw faces on miniature pumpkins with marking pens. Then have them write about their drawings, describing their pumpkins.
2. Wash, dry, roast, and eat the seeds from the pumpkin the class carved. Have each child write a cinquain, diamante, or concrete poem about the seeds.
3. Watch the video *Pumpkin Circle* (1997), which is about growing pumpkins. A book by the same title is also available (Levenson, 1999).
4. As a class, plant pumpkin seeds in pots or in the school garden. Visit the website **www.pumpkincircle.com** to get free pumpkin seeds (also available at **www.burpee.com**) and for information and activities, including how to make a root-viewing chamber.
5. Read books about pumpkins, including *Pumpkins* (Ray, 1992), *Pumpkin, Pumpkin* (Titherington, 1986), *The Pumpkin Patch* (King, 1990), and *The Pumpkin Blanket* (Zagwyn, 1995).

Children's Books and Films

Aardema, V. (1985). *Why mosquitoes buzz in people's ears.* New York: Dial.
Aliki. (1988). *Corn is maize.* New York: Harper & Row.
Ancona, G. (1993). *Pablo remembers: The fiesta of the Day of the Dead.* New York: Lothrop, Lee & Shepard.
Crowe, R. (1964). *Clyde monster.* New York: Dutton.

de Paola, T. (1978). *The popcorn book.* New York: Holiday House.

Earl, A., & Sensier, D. (1995). *Traditions around the world: Masks.* New York: Thomson Learning.

Ehlert, L. (1991). *Red leaf, yellow leaf.* New York: Harcourt Brace Jovanovich.

Flora. (1989). *Feathers like a rainbow: An Amazon Indian tale.* New York: Harper & Row.

Greene, C. (1990). *The thirteen days of Halloween.* New York: Children's Press.

Hancock, S. (1983). *Esteban and the ghost.* New York: Dial.

Hirschi, R. (1991). *Fall.* New York: Dutton.

Hopkins, L. B. (1974). *Hey-how for Halloween.* New York: Harcourt Brace Jovanovich.

King, E. (1990). *The pumpkin patch.* New York: Dutton.

Krull, K. (1994). *Maria Molina and the Days of the Dead.* New York: Macmillan.

Levenson, G. (1999). *Pumpkin circle.* Berkeley, CA: Tricycle Press.

Livingston, M. C. (1989). *Halloween poems.* New York: Holiday House.

Mayer, M. (1968). *There's a nightmare in my closet.* New York: Dial.

Prelutsky, J. (1977). *It's Halloween.* New York: Greenwillow.

Pumpkin circle [Film]. (1997). Available from Pumpkin Circle Project/Informed Democracy.

Ray, M. (1992). *Pumpkins.* New York: Harcourt Brace Jovanovich.

Ross, P. (1991). *M and M and the Halloween monster.* New York: Viking.

Ross, S. (1994). *Shakespeare & Macbeth: The story behind the play.* New York: Viking.

Selsam, M. (1976). *Popcorn.* New York: Morrow.

Sendak, M. (1963). *Where the wild things are.* New York: Harper & Row.

Simon, S. (1993). *Autumn across America.* New York: Hyperion Books.

Titherington, J. (1986). *Pumpkin, pumpkin.* New York: Greenwillow.

Udry, J. (1957). *A tree is nice.* New York: Harper & Row.

Wall, L. M. (1991). *Judge Rabbit and the tree spirit: A folktale from Cambodia.* New York: Children's Book Press.

Zagwyn, D. T. (1995). *The pumpkin blanket.* Berkeley, CA: Tricycle Press.

ZEA [Film]. (1982). Available from National Film Board of Canada.

Websites

The Popcorn Institute provides an encyclopedia of popcorn—history, science, and anything else you want to know at **www.popcorn.org:80/mpmain.htm.**

To get free pumpkin seeds, go to **www.pumpkincircle.com** or **www.burpee.com.** The Pumpkin Circle website also contains teaching ideas, resources, and links to other sites.

 **We're All Pilgrims**

Language and Literacy Experiences

Oral Histories

- *Interviews:* Students ask parents or grandparents about the countries of origin of their families. Questions to ask: "Where were you born?" "Where were your parents born?" "When did they come to United States?" "How old were they?" "Why did they leave their country?" "What was life like in the native country?" "How was it like/unlike life in the United Sates?" "Tell any special memories." Read *Grandfather's Journey* (Say, 1993), a story about Japanese American immigration.

- *Family Trees:* Using the information from the oral histories, students write their family memoirs. Read *Faraway Home* (Kurtz, 2000).

- *Map of Where We're All From:* On a wall-sized world map, children locate and label where their grandparents, parents, and other relatives are from. Then they make a border around the map with photographs or drawings of themselves. Their pictures can be connected to their families' countries of origins on the map with yarn and pins.

Documentary Interviews

- *Role-Playing:* Each child chooses a family member who came from another country and finds out some interesting facts about him or her. In pairs, children take turns role-playing their family members and interviewing them, like they're TV reporters. Read *The Lotus Seed* (Garland, 1993), which is about a Vietnamese woman who brings an important seed with her to the United States.
- *Videotaping:* Videotape students' interviews and create a documentary about immigration, emphasizing how we're all pilgrims.

Curriculum Drama

- *Ellis Island:* Students split into two groups: one portrays the staff at Ellis Island and the other portrays immigrants from different countries. Turn the room into Ellis Island with signs: "Medical Exams," "Money Exchange," and the like. The "immigrants" arrive and go through the process of entering the United States, which is run by the "staff." Then students switch roles, so everyone plays both roles. Students discuss and write about their experiences. Read *I Was Dreaming to Come to America: Memories from the Ellis Island Oral History Project* (Lawlor, 1995); *Ellis Island: Doorway to Freedom* (Kroll, 1995); *Ellis Island: New Hope in a New Land* (Jacobs, 1990); or *A Picnic in October* (Bunting, 1999).
- *The First Thanksgiving:* Younger students can dress as Pilgrims and Native Americans, decorate the room (e.g., with dried corn and cornstalks), set a table (e.g., make placemats and centerpieces), and prepare food: raw vegetables, simple batter bread and butter, popcorn, and vegetable soup. Read *Across the Wide Dark Sea: The Mayflower Journey* (Van Leeuwen, 1995); *Sarah Morton's Day: A Day in the Life of a Pilgrim Girl* (Waters, 1989); or *The First Thanksgiving Feast* (Anderson, 1989).

Lesson Plan: *Memory Boxes*

Level: Middle through upper grades

Purpose: Discuss, write, and fill a box based on family experiences.

Teaching Sequence:

1. Using family oral interviews as a basis for discussion, ask: "Where did they come from?" "What was the country they left like?" "Why did your family leave that country?" "Describe a special family memory of that country."
2. Record children's responses on chartpaper, using a large grid:

	We're All Pilgrims			
	Europe	Africa	Asia	The Americas
Describe country				
Reasons for leaving				
Special memories				

3. Discuss differences and similarities among children's family experiences.

4. Ask children to think about what special memories or things they would take with them if they were to leave their homes now. Discuss in groups.
5. Make folded boxes out of construction paper, or find an interesting box.
6. Have children decorate their boxes with labels and drawings of things they would take and draw and cut out things to put inside their boxes.

Extending Activities:
1. Children write about leaving a country, based on their experience or that of someone in their family. Write the account as a story or in journal form.
2. Show the film (16 mm or video) *Molly's Pilgrim* (1985; 24 min.).

Lesson Plan: *Family Tree*

Level: All grades

Purpose: Write about family experiences.

Teaching Sequence:
1. Read and discuss *Me and My Family Tree* (Sweeney, 1999).
2. Have each child "grow" his or her own family tree using this frame:

Family Tree

Grandmother & Grandfather   Grandmother & Grandfather

Mother   Father

Sisters   Me   Brothers

My Family Story

3. Send home directions telling family members that they can help students fill in the frame and provide dates, facts, anecdotal information, and photographs.
4. Have primary-level students illustrate their family trees by drawing pictures or pasting photographs of family members on them. Students should label each drawing or photo with the person's name, and at the bottom of the family tree (under *My Family Story*), students should write a sentence or two about their families. For younger students, the teacher can take dictation and add this information to each student's family tree. Middle elementary through middle school students can add more information about each family member, such as his or her date and place of birth, and write a few sentences to a paragraph about the individual. Older students can write extended stories about their families.

Extending Activities:
1. Consult the following books for information about family trees and genealogies: *Where Did You Get Those Eyes?* (Cooper, 1988), *Through the Eyes of Your Ancestors* (Taylor, 1999), and *The Great Ancestor Hunt* (Perl, 1989).
2. Read *Family Pictures: Cuadros de familia* (Lomas Garza, 1990). Then every month, have each child write about a family event, draw a picture about it, and save it in a folder. Publish all the writings and drawings as a book at the end of the schoolyear.
3. Host a Family Day, in which you invite family members to school. Have children share their family trees and family stories by displaying these projects on a bulletin board.
4. Have upper elementary and middle school students create HyperStudio autobiographies (see Chapter 13).

Children's Books and Films

Aliki. (1998). *Marianthe's story: Painted words Spoken memories.* New York: Greenwillow.

Anderson, J. (1989). *The first Thanksgiving feast.* Boston: Houghton Mifflin.

Atkin, S. B. (1993). *Voices from the fields: Children of immigrant farmworkers tell their story.* Boston: Little, Brown.

Bunting, E. (1988). *How many days to America? A Thanksgiving story.* New York: Clarion.

Bunting, E. (1994). *A day's work.* New York: Clarion.

Bunting, E. (1999). *A picnic in October.* San Diego: Harcourt Brace Jovanovich.

Cohen, B. (1983). *Molly's pilgrim.* New York: Lothrop, Lee & Shepard.

Cooper, K. (1988). *Where did you get those eyes?* New York: Walker.

Friedman, R. (1980). *Immigrant kids.* New York: Dutton.

Garland, S. (1993). *The lotus seed.* New York: Harcourt Brace Jovanovich.

Groff, N. (1993). *Where the river runs: A portrait of a refugee family.* Boston: Little, Brown.

Jacobs, W. (1990). *Ellis Island: New hope in a new land.* New York: Scribner's.

Kroll, S. (1991). *Mary McLean and the St. Patrick's Day parade.* New York: Scholastic.

Kroll, S. (1995). *Ellis Island: Doorway to freedom.* New York: Holiday House.

Kurtz, J. (2000). *Faraway home.* New York: Harcourt Brace Jovanovich.

Laden, N. (1998). *My family tree.* San Francisco: Chronicle.

Lawlor, V. (Ed.). (1995). *I was dreaming to come to America: Memories from the Ellis Island oral history project.* New York: Viking.

Lee, M. G. (1999). *F is for fabuloso.* New York: Avon.

Lomas Garza, C. (1990). *Family pictures: Cuadros de familia.* New York: Children's Book Press.

Lord, B. B. (1983). *In the year of the boar and Jackie Robinson.* New York: Harper & Row.

McKay, L. (2000). *Journey home.* New York: Lee & Low.

Molly's Pilgrim [Film]. (1985). Distributed by Phoenix Films.

Munoz, P. (2000). *Esperanza rising.* New York: Scholastic.

Perl, L. (1989). *The great ancestor hunt.* New York: Clarion.

Rosenberg, L. (1999). *The silence in the mountains.* New York: Orchard.

Sandler, M. W. (1995). *Immigrants.* New York: HarperCollins.

Say, A. (1993). *Grandfather's journey.* Boston: Houghton Mifflin.

Surat, M. (1983). *Angel child, dragon child.* New York: Carnival/Raintree.

Sweeney, J. (1999). *Me and my family tree.* New York: Crown.

Taylor, M. (1999). *Through the eyes of your ancestors.* Boston: Houghton Mifflin.

Van Leeuwen, J. (1995). *Across the wide dark sea: The Mayflower journey.* New York: Dial.

Waters, K. (1989). *Sarah Morton's Day: A day in the life of a Pilgrim girl.* New York: Scholastic.

Winter, J. (1992). *Klara's new world.* New York: Knopf.

Websites

Students can see if their family names are included on the American Immigrant Wall of Honor at **www.wallofhonor.com** or pass through Ellis Island Online, where they can explore the immigration museum at **www.ellisisland.org**. Current photos of Ellis Island are available at **www.icgnet.com/users/phil/ruins/ellis/index.html**.

Visit the National Genealogical Society at **www.ngsgenealogy.org**.

December Celebrations

Language and Literacy Experiences

Sharing Family Experiences

■ *Discuss:* Students talk about different types and ways of celebrating this time of the year (e.g., Hanukkah, Christmas, Kwanzaa). Do a "word wall" of different celebrations, noting how individual families celebrate each.

- *Write Memoirs:* Children do a cluster of ideas about special memories of celebrations as a basis for writing their memoirs.
- *Read: Too Many Tamales* (Soto, 1993); *Christmas Tree Memories* (Aliki, 1991); *Elijah's Angels: A Story for Chanukah and Christmas* (Rosen, 1992); *Tree of Cranes* (Say, 1991); or *Seven Candles for Kwanzaa* (Pinkney, 1993).

Reading and Writing for Information

- *Doing Research:* Children go to the library and find books on these celebrations for reading aloud, self-selected reading, and reading for information—for example, *Light the Candles! Beat the Drums!* (Sarnoff & Ruffin, 1979).
- *Chart Information:* Make a large wall chart on butcher paper about each celebration and how members of the class might celebrate:

	Hanukkah	Christmas	Kwanzaa
Who			
What			
Why			
How			
Where			

- *Celebration Posters:* In small groups, children create posters with information and illustrations about celebrations, based on their own family experiences and what they've learned reading. Groups share posters with the class.
- *"Big Book of Celebrations":* Bind students' celebration posters into a "big book" or make a book of writing and drawings about celebrations.

Reading and Writing Poetry

- *Read Poetry on All Celebrations: Celebrations* (Livingston, 1985); *Poems for Seasons and Celebrations* (Cole, 1961).
- *Write Poetry about Family Celebrations:* Children write free verses, patterns, or name poems (i.e., write the name of a holiday vertically on the left side of the paper, and add a phrase beginning with each letter).

Lesson Plan: *Celebration Filmstrips*

Level: Primary through upper grades

Purpose: Talk, read, draw, and write to create celebration filmstrips.

Teaching Sequence:
1. In cooperative groups of four to five, children brainstorm ideas for making draw-on filmstrips about celebrations with several options:
   - *Celebration Poem or Song:* Students choose their favorites and write and illustrate a few lines or stanzas on each filmstrip frame (e.g., "The Night Before Christmas"). Sources of poems are *Las Navidades: Popular Christmas Songs from Latin America* (Delacre, 1990) and *Poems for Jewish Holidays* (Livingston, 1986).
   - *Celebration Memoirs:* Students show the sequence of events of their special memories, adding narration to go with all frames.
   - *All about a Celebration:* On all frames, students illustrate things about the celebration, including information about it as the narration.
   - *Create a Celebration:* Children imagine and plan their own special celebrations.
2. Each group uses a filmstrip gauge (see Chapter 6) to draft drawings for each frame in sequence, with narration, sound effects, or music to go with it.

3. When the drafts are complete, children take blank filmstrip stock and tape over their filmstrip drafts. For blank filmstrip stock, (1) clean off old filmstrips, 35 mm negative strips, or 35 mm rolls of film in a solution of bleach and water, or (2) order it from a film supply company (e.g., Christy's Film Supply, Burbank, CA, 818-845-1755). Children can use permanent marking pens on acetate to trace over drawings (e.g., Staedtler Lumocolor 8313 permanent thin-tip markers).
4. The groups present their filmstrips. Narration, sound effects, or music can be live or taped.

Extending Activities:
1. *World Premiere of Celebration Filmstrips:* Children plan and host a premiere for other classes and parents, making posters, writing announcements (which can be delivered via loud speaker or computer bulletin boards), and drawing and writing invitations. Show the filmstrips in a darkened room or auditorium. Serve popcorn. Give Participation Awards to everyone.
2. *Make More Filmstrips, Films, Slides, or Transparencies:* Students draw on 16 mm films, slides, or transparencies (see Chapter 6) to illustrate other themes, using poetry, stories, or personal experiences.

Lesson Plan: *Celebrating Sadako's Life*

Level: Middle through upper grades

Purpose: Write a letter about a class project.

Teaching Sequence:
1. Read *Sadako* (Coerr, 1993), the story of Sadako Sasaki, a girl who developed leukemia in 1955 from the effects of radiation caused by the bombing of Hiroshima, Japan, in 1945. Her best friend reminded her of the Japanese legend that upon folding a thousand paper cranes, she would be granted her wish to get well. Sadako died before she could do so, but today, people all over the world fold garlands of cranes and send them to a statue of her in Hiroshima's Peace Park.
2. Discuss the book, asking students to share how they feel about the story of Sadako. Record their feelings on a "word wall."
3. Teach students how to fold a paper crane, and as a class begin making a garland of a thousand paper cranes. Ask other classes and family members to help. For information, consult a book about how to create origami or watch the video *How to Fold a Paper Crane.* Or call The Sadako Project (1-800-827-0949), and someone will send you directions and a piece of origami paper. You can also visit the project's website at **www.sadako.com.**
4. Do a minilesson on letter writing, and then write a class letter about the project and students' feelings about Sadako and her story. Send the letter with the crane garland to this address: Office of the Mayor, City of Hiroshima, 6-34 Kokutaiji-Machi, 1 Chome Naka-ku, Hiroshima 730 Japan.

Extending Activities:
1. Read more books about these topics:
   • Sadako: *Sadako and the Thousand Paper Cranes* (Coerr, 1998) and *Children of the Paper Crane: The Story of Sadako Sasaki and Her Struggle with the A-Bomb Disease* (Nasu, 1991)

- Paper cranes: *The Paper Crane* (Bang, 1987) and *Tree of Cranes* (Say, 1993)
- Hiroshima: *Hiroshima No Pika* (Maruki, 1982), *Shin's Tricycle* (Kodama, 1995), and *Hiroshima* (Yep, 1996)

2. Watch and discuss the video *Sadako and the Thousand Paper Cranes* (1990). (See Chapter 6 for guidelines on film study.)

Children's Books and Films

Aliki. (1991). *Christmas tree memories*. New York: HarperCollins.

Ancona, G. (1995). *Fiesta U.S.A.* New York: Lodestar.

Bang, M. (1987). *The paper crane*. New York: Greenwillow.

Baylor, B. (1986). *I'm in charge of celebrations*. New York: Scribner's.

Chocolate, D. (1992). *My first Kwanzaa book*. New York: Scholastic.

Coerr, E. (1993). *Sadako*. New York: Dell.

Coerr, E. (1998). *Sadako and the thousand paper cranes*. New York: Putnam.

Cole, W. (1961). *Poems for seasons and celebrations*. New York: World.

Delacre, L. (1990). *Las navidades: Popular Christmas songs from Latin America*. New York: Scholastic.

Drucker, M. (1992). *Grandma's latkes*. New York: Trumpet Club.

Foster, J. (1997). *Let's celebrate: Festival poems*. New York: Oxford University Press.

Howard, E. (1989). *Chita's Christmas tree*. New York: Bradbury Books.

How to fold a paper crane [Film]. (1990). Available from The Sadako Project/Informed Democracy.

Hoyt-Goldsmith, D. (1993). *Celebrating Kwanzaa*. New York: Holiday House.

Kodama, T. (1995). *Shin's tricycle*. New York: Walker.

Livingston, M. C. (1985). *Celebrations*. New York: Holiday House.

Livingston, M. C. (1986). *Poems for Jewish holidays*. New York: Holiday House.

Manushkin, F. (1989). *Latkes and applesauce: A Hanukkah story*. New York: Scholastic.

Maruki, T. (1982). *Hiroshima no pika*. New York: Lothrop, Lee & Shepard.

Nasu, M. (1991). *Children of the paper crane: The story of Sadako Sasaki and her struggle with the A-bomb disease* (E. W. Baldwin, S. L. Leeper, and K. Yoshida, Trans.). Armonk, NY: M. E. Sharpe.

Pinkney, A. (1993). *Seven candles for Kwanzaa*. New York: Dial.

Riehecky, J. (1993). *Kwanzaa*. New York: Children's Press.

Rosen, M. (1992). *Elijah's angels: A story for Chanukah and Christmas*. New York: Harcourt Brace Jovanovich.

Ryder, J. (1994). *First grade elves*. Mahwah, NJ: Troll.

Sadako and the thousand paper cranes [Film]. (1990). Available from The Sadako Project/ Informed Democracy.

Sarnoff, J., & Ruffin, R. (1979). *Light the candles! Beat the drums!* New York: Scribner's.

Say, A. (1991). *Tree of cranes*. Boston: Houghton Mifflin.

Soto, G. (1993). *Too many tamales*. New York: Putnam's.

Spier, P. (1983). *Peter Spier's Christmas!* New York: Doubleday.

Yep, L. (1996). *Hiroshima*. New York: HarperCollins.

Websites

Information about December celebrations all over the world (from Kwanzaa to Hogmanay to Las Posadas), celebrations throughout the year on a World Holiday Calendar, and things for children to celebrate everyday can be found at **www.emg. com/celebration/celebrations.html**.

Contact The Sadako Project at **www.sadako.com** for directions on folding paper cranes and a piece of origami paper.

January   Winter

Language and Literacy Experiences

Writing and Illustrating Images

- *Talk about Winter Images:* Children talk about gray skies, leafless trees, brown grass, snow, and so on.
- *"Word Wall":* Students creates a "word wall" of winter images based on their experiences or in response to words and illustrations from the two books.
- *Write and Illustrate Winter Images:* Children write haiku, cinquain, poetry, prose, or captions and illustrate them using tempera paint (white paint on dark paper, cotton balls for gluing, torn paper collage as used by Keats), tissue paper applied with starch, or construction paper.

Read about and Dramatize Different New Year's Celebrations

- *Read: New Year's Poems* (Livingston, 1987); *All in a Day* (Anno, 1986); *Lion Dancer: Ernie Wan's Chinese New Year* (Waters & Slovenz-Low, 1990); *Chinese New Year* (Brown, 1987); *Chinese New Year's Dragon* (Sing, 1992); *Chin Chiang and the Dragon Dance* (Wallace, 1984); *Hoan Anh: A Vietnamese-American Boy* (Hoyt-Goldsmith, 1992); *Dara's Cambodian New Year* (Chiemruom, 1992); or *Dumpling Soup* (Rattigan, 1998).
- *New Year's Celebrations Day:* Children form groups, choosing one type of New Year's celebration to read more about. Then they choose one aspect of it to dramatize through reader's theater, role-playing, puppets, story dramatization, music, or dance. All groups share their celebrations on one day.

Lesson Plan: *Snowy Days and Evenings*

Level: Primary grades (Plan A) through upper grades (Plan B)

Purpose: Read and respond to literature through talking, writing, and drawing.

Teaching Sequence:

Plan A: Primary Grades

1. Read aloud *The Snowy Day* (Keats, 1962), about a young child's experiences with snow.
2. Discuss the book using aesthetic, open-ended questions and prompts such as these:

   What did you think of the book?
   What was your favorite part?
   What experiences have you had in the snow?
   What would you like to do in the snow?

3. Using the heading "Snowy Days," create a "word wall" on chartpaper by writing down the children's ideas.
4. Using the "word wall" for ideas, have children write about snowy days. They can illustrate their writing by drawing pictures or by using clip art or other graphics software. Emerging writers can add their names to their work and then give dictation to the teacher to write captions on their pictures.

Plan B: Primary through Upper Grades*

1. Read aloud a single-edition illustrated text of Robert Frost's poem *Stopping by Woods on a Snowy Evening* (e.g., Frost, 1978). Then discuss the poem, especially the images and feelings of winter that Frost creates.
2. Have each student write a paragraph about the images and feelings he or she had while listening to the poem.
3. Ask students to create visual images for the individual lines of the poem using crayons, markers, watercolors, or collage. Each line of the poem and its illustration should be on a separate page. Using a similar format, students could create film-strips of the poem, as well, allotting one frame per line/illustration (see Chapter 6).
4. Help students compile their separate pages of illustrated lines from the poem into their own books (see Chapter 7) or videos (see Chapter 6).

Extending Activities:
Plan A: Primary Grades

1. Read more books about snow: *Katy and the Big Snow* (Burton, 1943), *Black Snowman* (Menendez, 1989), *The First Snowfall* (Rockwell, 1987), and *Owl Moon* (Yolen, 1988).
2. Have students create language experience stories after one of these activities:
   Making "angels" in the snow or in a sandbox (if snow isn't available)
   Making snow cones with crushed ice
   Creating a snow scene or a snowperson by gluing white packing peanuts (otherwise known as "ghost poopies") on blue or black paper
   Cutting out paper snowflakes (see *I Am Snow* [Marzollo, 1998])
3. Do a KWL chart on snow and use books for information: *Snow Is Falling* (Branley, 2000), *Snowflake Bentley* (Martin, 1998), and *Snow and Ice* (Steele, 1998).
4. Watch the movie *The Snowman* (1982), and read the book it was based on, *The Snowman* (Briggs, 1978). Then as a class, make a video or filmstrip about an adventure in the snow (see Chapter 6).

Plan B: Primary through Upper Grades

1. Read other poems by Robert Frost, such as *Birches* (Frost, 1988), *A Swinger of Birches* (Frost, 1982), and *You Come Too* (Frost, 1959).
2. Read other poems about snow: *Winter Eyes* (Florian, 1999) and *It's Snowing, It's Snowing* (Prelutsky, 1984).
3. Have students make poetry posters by illustrating their own poems on tagboard or chartpaper.
4. Have the class sing and dance to a poem. To do so, pick a familiar tune—perhaps "London Bridge" or Twinkle, Twinkle Little Star"—and adapt it to fit the words of a simple poem. Once the students are comfortable with singing the poem, have them create movements to dance to it.

Lesson Plan: *"I Have a Dream"*

Level: Primary through upper grades

Purpose: Read, talk, and write in response to ideas of Martin Luther King, Jr.

*Thanks to Gail Schack for this idea.

Teaching Sequence:
1. In connection with celebration of the Martin Luther King, Jr., holiday, read about his life and ideas: *I Have a Dream: The Life and Words of Martin Luther King, Jr.* (Haskins, 1993).
2. Ask students to respond to his ideas in class and small cooperative group discussions.
3. Ask students to consider what their dreams for the future are, and record them on a word wall cluster for the whole class: "I HAVE A DREAM."
4. Students write clusters of dreams, using the class word wall as a model and choosing one or a few words to expand on in writing (a few sentences or up to a paragraph). For emerging writers, the teacher takes dictation.
5. Students illustrate one or some of their dreams and display their drawings with their writing on a class bulletin board: "I HAVE A DREAM."

Extending Activities:
1. Display students' writing and drawing on a class bulletin board ("I HAVE A DREAM"), or bind them into a class book for the classroom library.
2. Read the following: *A Picture Book of Martin Luther King, Jr.* (Adler, 1989); *Martin Luther King Day* (Lowrey, 1987); *Meet Martin Luther King* (DeKay, 1969); *My Life with Martin Luther King, Jr.* (King, 1993); or *Martin Luther King, Jr., and the Freedom Movement* (Patterson, 1989).
3. Create a timeline and mural of major events and ideas in the life of King.
4. Read about other famous African Americans. Then compare their lives and ideas to those of Martin Luther King, Jr. (e.g., *Malcolm X: By Any Means Necessary* [Myers, 1993]) or with those of leaders of other minority groups in the United States (e.g., *Caesar Chavez* [Concord, 1992] and *Cesar Chavez* [Franchure, 1988], the Chicano American union leader).
5. Read aloud *The Dream Keeper and Other Poems* (Hughes, 1994).
6. Read and do a reader's theater or chorale reading of *I Am a Man: Ode to Martin Luther King, Jr.* (Merriam, 1971).

Children's Books and Films

Adler, D. (1989). *A picture book of Martin Luther King, Jr.* New York: Holiday House.
Anno. (1986). *All in a day.* New York: Philomel.
Bauer, C. F. (Ed.). (1986). *Snow day: Stories and poems.* New York: Lippincott.
Branley, F. (2000). *Snow is falling.* New York: HarperCollins.
Bray, R. L. (1995). *Martin Luther King.* New York: Greenwillow.
Briggs, R. (1978). *The snowman.* New York: Random House.
Brown, K. (1995). *Martin Luther King: His life and legacy.* New York: Millbrook.
Brown, T. (1987). *Chinese New Year.* New York: Holt.
Burton, V. L. (1943). *Katy and the big snow.* Boston: Houghton Mifflin.
Chaffin, L. (1980). *We be warm till springtime comes.* New York: Macmillan.
Chiemruom, S. (1992). *Dara's Cambodian New Year.* Cleveland: Modern Curriculum Press.
Concord, B. (1988). *Caesar Chavez.* New York: Chelsea.
DeKay, J. (1969). *Meet Martin Luther King.* New York: Random House.
Franchure, R. (1988). *Cesar Chavez.* New York: Harper & Row.
Florian, D. (1999). *Winter eyes.* New York: Greenwillow.
Frost, R. (1959). *You come too: Favorite poems for young people.* New York: Henry Holt.
Frost, R. (1978). *Stopping by woods on a snowy evening.* New York: Dutton.

Frost, R. (1982). *A swinger of birches: Poems of Robert Frost for young people.* Owings Mills, MD: Stemmer House.

Frost, R. (1988). *Birches.* New York: Henry Holt.

Haskins, J. (1993). *I have a dream: The life and words of Martin Luther King, Jr.* Highland Park, NY: Millbrook.

Hirschi, R. (1990). *Winter.* New York: Dutton.

Hoyt-Goldsmith, D. (1992). *Hoan Anh: A Vietnamese-American boy.* New York: Holiday House.

Hughes, L. (1994). *The dream keeper and other poems.* New York: Knopf.

Keats, E. J. (1962). *The snowy day.* New York: Viking.

King, C. S. (1993). *My life with Martin Luther King, Jr.* New York: Holt.

Kroll, V. (1994). *The seasons and someone.* New York: Harcourt Brace Jovanovich.

Livingston, M. C. (1987). *New Year's poems.* New York: Holiday House.

Lowrey, L. (1987). *Martin Luther King Day.* Minneapolis: Carolrhoda.

Martin, J. B. (1998). *Snowflake Bentley.* Boston: Houghton Mifflin.

Marzollo, J. (1998). *I am snow.* New York: Scholastic.

Menendez, P. (1989). *Black snowman.* New York: Scholastic.

Merriam, E. (1971). *I am a man: Ode to Martin Luther King, Jr.* New York: Doubleday.

Myers, W. D. (1993). *Malcolm X: By any means necessary.* New York: Scholastic.

Patterson, L. (1989). *Martin Luther King, Jr., and the freedom movement.* New York: Facts on File.

Prelutsky, J. (1984). *It's snowing! It's snowing!* New York: Greenwillow.

Radin, R. (1982). *A winter place.* Boston: Little, Brown.

Rattigan, J. K. (1998). *Dumpling soup.* New York: Little, Brown.

Ringgold, F. (1995). *My dream of Martin Luther King.* New York: Crown.

Rockwell, A. (1987). *The first snowfall.* New York: Macmillan.

Rogasky, B. (1994). *Winter poems.* New York: Scholastic.

Sing, R. (1992). *Chinese New Year's dragon.* Cleveland: Modern Curriculum Press.

Snowman, The [Film]. (1982). Available from the National Film Board of Canada.

Steele, P. (1998). *Snow and ice.* Austin, TX: Raintree Steck–Vaughn.

Wallace, I. (1984). *Chin Chiang and the dragon dance.* New York: Atheneum.

Waters, K., & Slovenz-Low, M. (1990). *Lion dancer: Ernie Wan's Chinese New Year.* New York: Scholastic.

Yolen, J. (1988). *Owl moon.* New York: Philomel.

Yolen, J. (1998). *Snow, snow: Winter poems for children.* Honesdale, PA: Wordsong.

Websites

Children from around the world tell how they celebrate the New Year at **wilstar.net/newyear.htm.**

February   Black History Month

Language and Literacy Experiences

Read Biographies

- *Read Aloud and Discuss: A Weed Is a Flower: The Life of George Washington Carver* (Aliki, 1988), about the man who demonstrated multiple ways to use sweet potatoes and peanuts; *Rosa Parks* (Greenfield, 1973), about the woman who sparked the civil rights movement; and *Harriet Tubman and Black History Month* (Carter, 1990), an introduction to biographies of African Americans and Black History Month.

■ *Literature Groups:* These are good books for literature groups to choose, read, and do projects on: *Amos Fortune, Free Man* (Yates, 1967); *Anthony Burns: The Defeat and Triumph of a Fugitive Slave* (Hamilton, 1988); *Matthew Henson, Explorer* (Gilman, 1988); *Thurgood Marshall: A Life for Justice* (Haskins, 1992); *Ray Charles* (Mathis, 1973); *Duke Ellington* (Pinkney, 1998); *Black Stars in Orbit: NASA's African American Astronauts* (Burns & Miles, 1995); *Coming Home: From the Life of Langston Hughes* (Cooper, 1994); and *Story Painter: The Life of Jacob Lawrence* (Duggleby, 1998).

Reader's Theater

■ *Scripts:* Students adapt reader's theater scripts based on the words of African Americans at different periods of history. Sources include *To Be a Slave* (Lester, 1968); *Rosa Parks: My Story* (Parks/Haskins, 1994); *Shirley Chisholm: Teacher and Congresswoman* (Scheader, 1990); *Malcolm X* (Adoff, 1970); *Jesse Jackson* (McKissack, 1989); and *The Black Americans: A History in Their Own Words, 1619–1983* (Meltzer, 1984); *Frederick Douglass: In His Own Words* (Meltzer, 1995); *Escape from Slavery: The Boyhood of Frederick Douglass in His Own Words* (McCurdy, 1994); and *The Underground Railroad* (Bial, 1995).

Curriculum Drama

■ *Recreating History:* Students read about and dramatize scenes from important moments in African American history. Sources include *Runaway Slave: The Story of Harriet Tubman* (McGovern, 1968), which is about helping other slaves to freedom; *The Freedom Ship of Robert Smalls* (Meriwether, 1971), about a slave who hijacked a ship and with a slave crew sailed it to freedom during the Civil War; and *Rosa Parks and the Montgomery Bus Boycott* (Celsi, 1991), about the famous incident on the bus.

■ *Read and Play:* Children read and play scenes. Sources include *Langston: A Play* (Davis, 1982), about the African American poet Langston Hughes; *Take a Walk in Their Shoes* (Turner, 1989), about the lives of African Americans; and *Plays of Black Americans: The Black Experience in America, Dramatized for Young People* (Kamerman, 1994).

Black History Timeline Mural

■ *Create a Timeline:* Children in groups research different periods of African American history and make an illustrated timeline on a wall-length mural of butcher paper, adding paintings, cut-out figures, photographs, writing, and artifacts.

■ *Display on Tables beneath the Timeline:* Collect books about African Americans and black history and related student writing, art, and projects.

Lesson Plan: *Black History Newspaper*

Level: Middle grades through middle school

Purpose: Read, talk, write, and report on black history in a newspaper format.

Teaching Sequence:

1. After a period of reading, talking, writing, and doing projects on African American history, students plan a newspaper to report what they have discovered.

2. As a class, brainstorm ideas for sections and topics for each section. Record them on chartpaper, leaving space under each topic: "Articles," "Editorials," "Letters to Editor," "Sports," "Entertainment," "Book Reviews," "Cartoons & Comics," and "Classified Ads."
3. Small groups are formed and assigned sections. Groups brainstorm ideas, choose section editors, decide who will write what, and begin drafts.
4. In a final class discussion, each section leader shares topics and ideas, which the teach-er records on the chart under each section head. The chart is a working plan for the production of the newspaper. Note section editors and group members on the chart.

Extending Activities:
1. Students continue to read, write, illustrate, and produce the newspaper.
2. Use software designed for newspaper production and desktop publishing.
3. Read accounts of African American history: *The March on Washington* (Haskins, 1993); *Freedom's Children: Young Civil Rights Activists Tell Their Own Stories* (Levine, 1993); *Escape from Slavery: The Boyhood of Frederick Douglass in His Own Words* (Mc-Curdy, 1994); *The Civil Rights Movement in America from 1865 to the Present* (McKissack & McKissack, 1991); *A Long Hard Journey: The Story of the Pullman Porter* (McKissack & McKissack, 1989); *Now Is Your Time! The African-American Struggle for Freedom* (Myers, 1991).

Lesson Plan: *Video Biographies of African Americans*

Level: Middle grades through middle school

Purpose: Research, read, and write expository (autobiographical/biographical) texts in video script form or text for a HyperStudio project.

Teaching Sequence:
1. Read aloud picture book biographies of famous African Americans, such as Ruby Bridges: *The Story of Ruby Bridges* (Coles, 1995) and *Through My Eyes* (Bridges, 1999).
2. Have students form literature groups (see Chapter 7) and choose and read one or more biographies or autobiographies about African Americans. Encourage students to do additional research using sources such as reference books and the Internet. Have students share what they learn about these individuals with the class. To guide students' choices of people and books, prepare a collection in the classroom or library. See the list of Children's Books and Films at the end of this section for some possible titles.
3. Have each literature group write a video script or HyperStudio text about their subject. (See Chapter 10 for ideas about writing biographies.)
4. Help each literature group make a video (see Chapter 6) or HyperStudio project (see Chapter 13) about their individual. To prepare, the group should gather props and costumes, select music, and rehearse. Use these projects to form a class collection of biographies of famous African Americans.

Extending Activities:
1. To get ideas about how to write the script for a biography, encourage students to watch biographical segments on The History Channel or the program "Biogra-phy" on A&E.

2. Have students create a HyperStudio project about several people from a single historical period, such as Ruby Bridges, Rosa Parks, and Martin Luther King, Jr., during the Civil Rights movement in the late 1950s and 1960s. More than one literature group could collaborate on such a project.
3. Hold a world premier during Black History Month to show students' videos or HyperStudio projects. Have students send out invitations to other classes as well as to their families and perhaps even members of the community. Students should also promote the event by sending an announcement or press release to the education editor of the local newspaper.
4. Read aloud and discuss *Zack* (Bell, 1999), which is about a boy who discovers his own heritage while writing a class history project.

Children's Books and Films

Adoff, A. (1970). *Malcolm X.* New York: Crowell.
Aliki. (1988). *A weed is a flower: The life of George Washington Carver.* New York: Simon & Schuster.
Bell, W. (1999). *Zack.* New York: Simon & Schuster.
Bial, R. (1995). *The underground railroad.* New York: Houghton Mifflin.
Bridges, R. (1999). *Through my eyes.* New York: Scholastic.
Burns, K., & Miles, W. (1995). *Black stars in orbit: NASA's African American astronauts.* New York: Harcourt Brace Jovanovich.
Carter, P. (1990). *Harriet Tubman and black history month.* Columbus, OH: Silver Press.
Celsi, T. (1991). *Rosa Parks and the Montgomery bus boycott.* New York: Milbrook.
Coles, R. (1995). *The story of Ruby Bridges.* New York: Scholastic.
Cooper, F. (1994). *Coming home: From the life of Langston Hughes.* New York: Philomel.
Curtis, C. P. (1995). *The Watsons go to Birimingham—1963.* New York: Delacorte.
Davis, O. (1982). *Langston: A play.* New York: Delacorte.
Duggleby, J. (1998). *Story painter: The life of Jacob Lawrence.* New York: Chronicle.
Edwards, P. D. (1997). *Barefoot: Escape on the underground railroad.* New York: HarperCollins.
Feelings, T. (1995). *The middle passage: White ship/black cargo.* New York: Dial.
Fox, P. (1973). *Slave dancer.* New York: Bradbury Books.
Gilman, M. (1988). *Matthew Henson, explorer.* New York: Chelsea House.
Greenfield, E. (1973). *Rosa Parks.* New York: Crowell.
Greenfield, E. (1989). *Nathaniel talking.* New York: Black Butterfly Children's Books.
Hamilton, V. (1988). *Anthony Burns: The defeat and triumph of a fugitive slave.* New York: Knopf.
Hamilton, V. (1993). *Many thousand gone: African Americans from slavery to freedom.* New York: Knopf.
Haskins, J. (1984). *Space challenger: The story of Guion Bluford.* Minneapolis: Carolrhoda.
Haskins, J. (1992). *Thurgood Marshall: A life for justice.* New York: Holt.
Haskins, J. (1993). *The march on Washington.* New York: HarperCollins.
Haskins, J. (1995). *Freedom rides: Journey for justice.* New York: Hyperion.
Hoobler, D., & Hoobler, T. (1995). *The African American family album.* New York: Oxford University Press.
Kamerman, S. (Ed.). (1994). *Plays of Black Americans: The Black experience in America, dramatized for young people.* Boston: Plays.
Lester, J. (Ed.). (1968). *To be a slave.* New York: Dial.
Lester, J. (1998). *Black cowboy, wild horses: A true story.* New York: Dial.
Levine, E. (1993). *Freedom's children: Young civil rights activists tell their own stories.* New York: Putnam's.
Mathis, S. B. (1973). *Ray Charles.* New York: Crowell.
McCurdy, M. (Ed.). (1994). *Escape from slavery: The boyhood of Frederick Douglass in his own words.* New York: Knopf.

McGovern, A. (1968). *Runaway slave: The story of Harriet Tubman.* New York: Four Winds.
McKissack, P. (1989). *Jesse Jackson.* New York: Scholastic.
McKissack, P., & McKissack, F. (1989). *A long hard journey: The story of the Pullman porter.* New York: Walker.
McKissack, P., & McKissack, F. (1991). *The civil rights movement in America from 1865 to the present.* New York: Children's Press.
McKissack, P., & McKissack, F. (1999). *Black hands, white sails: The story of African-American whalers.* New York: Scholastic.
Meltzer, M. (1984). *The Black Americans: A history in their own words, 1619–1983.* New York: Crowell.
Meltzer, M. (1995). *Frederick Douglass: In his own words.* New York: Harcourt Brace.
Meriwether, L. (1971). *The freedom ship of Robert Smalls.* New York: Prentice-Hall.
Myers, W. D. (1991). *Now is your time! The African-American struggle for freedom.* New York: HarperCollins.
Myers, W. D. (1993). *Brown angels: An album of pictures and verse.* New York: Harper & Row.
Myers, W. D. (1997). *Harlem.* New York: Scholastic.
Myers, W. D. (2000). *Malcom X: A fire burning brightly.* New York: HarperCollins.
Parks, R. (with J. Haskins). (1994). *Rosa Parks: My story.* New York: Dial.
Pinkney, A. D. (1998). *Duke Ellington.* New York: Hyperion.
Porter, C. (1994). *Meet Addy* (and other Addy books). New York: American Girl.
Ringgold, F. (1993). *Aunt Harriet's underground railroad in the sky.* New York: Crown.
Scheader, C. (1990). *Shirley Chisholm: Teacher and congresswoman.* Hillsdale, NJ: Enslow.
Turner, G. (1989). *Take a walk in their shoes.* New York: Cobblehill.
Yates, E. (1967). *Amos Fortune, free man.* New York: Dutton.

Websites

For information on African American history, culture, and current events, see **www. coax.net/people/lwf**. For a biography and list of the synthetic products developed by George Washington Carver, as well as a visit to the George Washington Carver National Monument, go to **www.lib.lsu.edu/lib/chem/display/carver.html**.

March   Women's History Month

Language and Literacy Experiences

Family Women's History

- *Interviews:* Each child interviews family members about women in his or her family: "Who were they?" "Where were they from?" "What did they do?" "What was their life like?"
- *Timelines:* Children create timelines of the lives of women in their families.
- *Scrapbooks:* Using black construction paper, each child makes a scrapbook about women in his or her family, including (for each woman) information, photographs, drawings, and mementos. Individual students' pages are assembled into a class scrapbook or mounted on a bulletin board.
- *Mother's Day in Class:* Children invite mothers or other women family members or friends to come to class to talk about their lives and those of other women in their families, describing backgrounds, jobs, and special talents.
- *Read Aloud:* The teacher reads aloud to students *Childtimes: A Three-Generation Memoir* (Greenfield & Little, 1979), an intergenerational childhood memoir by three African American women.

Reading Biographies, Scriptwriting, and Drama
- *Read Aloud:* The teacher reads aloud *Taking Flight: My Story* by *Vicki Van Meter* (Van Meter/Gurman, 1995), about a 12-year-old girl who piloted a plane across the Atlantic, or *Wilma Unlimited: How Wilma Rudolph Became the World's Fastest Woman* (Krull, 1996), about the great African American athlete.
- *Literature Groups:* Students in groups choose and read books such as *Queen Eleanor: Independent Spirit of the Medieval World* (Brooks, 1983); *Demeter's Daughters: The Women Who Founded America 1587–1787* (Williams, 1976); ·*Founding Mothers: Women of America in the Revolutionary Era* (De Pauw, 1994); *Susette La Flesche: Advocate for Native American Rights* (Brown, 1992); *The Last Princess: The Story of Princess Ka'iulani of Hawaii* (Stanley, 1991); *Louisa May: The World and Works of Louisa May Alcott* (Johnston, 1991); *Eleanor Roosevelt: A Life of Discovery* (Freedman, 1993); *Amelia Earhart* (Pearce, 1988); and *Women Astronauts: Aboard the Shuttle* (Fox, 1984).
- *Drama:* Each group writes and plays a scene in the life of a famous woman.

Women Visual and Performing Artists
- *Read:* The teacher reads aloud books such as *Inspirations: Stories about Women Artists* (Sills, 1989); *Visions: Stories about Women Artists* (Sills, 1993); *Frida Kahlo* (Turner, 1993); *Georgia O'Keeffe* (Turner, 1991); *An Actor's Life for Me!* (Gish/Lanes, 1987); *Barefoot Dancer: The Story of Isadora Duncan* (O'Connor, 1994); and *Big Star Fallin' Mama: Five Women in Black Music* (Jones, 1995).
- *Recreate:* Students do paintings and performances in the styles of women visual and performing artists (e.g., Georgia O'Keefe's paintings, Isadora Duncan's dancing).

Women's History Museum
- *Create a Museum:* Collect books about women, including student-written stories, and add student projects (writing and drawing, dioramas, posters, artifacts with labels and captions) about women's contributions to history.

Lesson Plan: *Woman of the Year*

Level: All grades

Purpose: Research, write, and illustrate a biography of a Woman of the Year.

Teaching Sequence:
1. Read excerpts from *Sisters in Strength: American Women Who Made a Difference* (McDonough, 2000), and then discuss these questions with students:
   What did you think of these stories?
   Why did the author choose these women to write about?
   How do you write a biography?
2. Do a "word wall" of student responses to the question about why the author chose these women to write about. Guide students to think about what makes someone successful or brave or famous.
3. Create a class poster of the information needed to write a biography:
   Name of person
   Dates of birth and death (if deceased)
   Childhood and family background
   Major life events and accomplishments

4. Show students a *Time* magazine that features a Person of the Year, and discuss why that individual was chosen. As a class, brainstorm a list of women that students think would be good candidates for Woman of the Year. Consider public figures as well as women the students know personally and admire.
5. Ask each child to pick a Woman of the Year to research and write about. Students should use the class poster to guide them in gathering information, and their research should include a range of sources: books, the Internet, and perhaps interviews, if they know their subjects.
6. After students have written their biographies, have them create simulated *Time* magazine covers featuring their individual choices for Woman of the Year. Then publish each student's biography as a magazine article about the subject's life.

Extending Activities:
1. Help students adapt their written Woman of the Year projects to HyperStudio projects (see Chapter 13).
2. Invite several women to speak to the class over a period of weeks as part of a Woman of the Year series.
3. Have students find out how many women have been chosen to be the Person of the Year on the cover of *Time* magazine. As a class, make a list of these individuals and why they were acknowledged. If any are still living, write to them and ask how their lives were affected by receiving this honor.

Lesson Plan: *Women's History Quilt*

Level: Middle through upper grades

Purpose: Read, talk, write, and draw about the lives of famous women.

Teaching Sequence:
1. Read aloud and discuss *Good Queen Bess: Queen Elizabeth I of England* (Stanley & Vennema, 1990).
2. Do a "word wall," clustering ideas from children about Queen Bess's characteristics.
3. Based on reading the biography of a famous woman, each child or children in cooperative groups create a cluster of ideas and images about her.
4. Based on their cluster of ideas, each child or group sketches a quilt square (12" × 12" is a good size) about their famous woman. The squares could be created by using liquid embroidery pens to draw on cloth (e.g., muslin); by gluing on appliqués of scraps of cloth, felt, yarn, buttons, feathers, and so on; or by using construction paper.

Extending Activities:
1. The quilt squares are sewn, stapled, or hole-punched and tied together with yarn to create a class women's history quilt.
2. Read books with quilt motifs: *Eight Hands Round: A Patchwork Alphabet* (Paul, 1991); *Tar Beach* (Ringgold, 1991); *The Josefina Story Quilt* (Coerr, 1986); *Sweet Clara and the Freedom Quilt* (Hopkinson, 1993); *Sam Johnson and the Blue Ribbon Quilt* (Ernst, 1983); *The Patchwork Quilt* (Flournoy, 1985); *The Keeping Quilt* (Polacco, 1988); *Tonight Is Carnaval* (Dorros, 1995); *The Canada Geese Quilt* (Kinsey-Warnock, 1989); *Nine in One Grr! Grr! A Folktale from the Hmong People of Laos*

(Xong, 1989); *The Quilt Story* (Johnston, 1985); *The Quilt* (Jonas, 1984); *The Whispering Cloth: A Refugee's Story* (Shea, 1995); and *Selina and the Bear Paw Quilt* (Smucker, 1996).

3. Read aloud *The Always Prayer Shawl* (Oberman, 1994), the story of a shawl that is passed down through several generations of Jewish men, which shows that textiles can be important to men as well as women.

Children's Books

Ashby, R. (Ed.). (1995). *Herstory: Women who changed the world.* New York: Viking.

Brooks, P. S. (1983). *Queen Eleanor: Independent spirit of the medieval world.* Philadelphia: Lippincott.

Brown, M. M. (1992). *Susette La Flesche: Advocate for Native American rights.* New York: Children's Press.

Coerr, E. (1986). *The Josefina story quilt.* New York: HarperCollins.

De Pauw, L. (1994). *Founding mothers: Women of America in the Revolutionary era.* Boston: Houghton Mifflin.

Dorros, A. (1995). *Tonight is Carnaval.* New York: Dutton.

Ernst, L. C. (1983). *Sam Johnson and the blue ribbon quilt.* New York: Lothrop, Lee & Shepard.

Flournoy, V. (1985). *The patchwork quilt.* New York: Dial.

Fox, M. V. (1984). *Women astronauts: Aboard the shuttle.* New York: Messner.

Freedman, R. (1993). *Eleanor Roosevelt: A life of discovery.* New York: Clarion.

Gish, L. (told to S. Lanes). (1987). *An actor's life for me!* New York: Viking.

Greenfield, E., & Little, L. J. (1979). *Childtimes: A three-generation memoir.* New York: Crowell.

Hopkinson, D. (1993). *Sweet Clara and the freedom quilt.* New York: Knopf.

Houston, G. (1992). *My Great Aunt Arizona.* New York: HarperCollins.

Johnston, N. (1991). *Louisa May: The world and works of Louisa May Alcott.* New York: Four Winds.

Johnston, T. (1985). *The quilt story.* New York: Putnam.

Jonas, A. (1984). *The quilt.* New York: Greenwillow.

Jones, H. (1995). *Big star fallin' Mama: Five women in Black music.* New York: Viking.

Kinsey-Warnock, N. (1989). *The Canada geese quilt.* New York: Cobblehill.

Klein, N. (1975). *Girls can be anything.* New York: Dutton.

Krull, K. (1996). *Wilma unlimited: How Wilma Rudolph became the world's fastest woman.* New York: Harcourt Brace Jovanovich.

McDonough, Y. Z. (2000). *Sisters in strength: American women who made a difference.* New York: Holt.

Oberman, S. (1994). *The always prayer shawl.* Honesdale, PA: Boyds Mills.

O'Connor, B. (1994). *Barefoot dancer: The story of Isadora Duncan.* Minneapolis: Carolrhoda.

Paul, A. W. (1991). *Eight hands round: A patchwork alphabet.* New York: HarperCollins.

Pearce, C. A. (1988). *Amelia Earhart.* New York: Facts on File.

Polacco, P. (1988). *The keeping quilt.* New York: Simon & Schuster.

Ringgold, F. (1991). *Tar beach.* New York: Crown.

Shea, P. D. (1995). *The whispering cloth: A refugee's story.* Honesdale, PA: Boyds Mill Press.

Sills, L. (1989). *Inspirations: Stories about women artists.* New York: Whitman.

Sills, L. (1993). *Visions: Stories about women artists.* New York: Whitman.

Smucker, B. (1996). *Selina and the bear paw quilt.* New York: Crown.

Stanley, D., & Vennema, P. (1990). *Good Queen Bess: Queen Elizabeth I of England.* New York: Four Winds.

Stanley, F. (1991). *The last princess: The story of Princess Ka'iulani of Hawaii.* New York: Four Winds.

Turner, R. (1991). *Georgia O'Keefe.* Boston: Little, Brown.

Turner, R. (1993). *Frida Kahlo.* Boston: Little, Brown.

Van Meter, V. (with D. Gurman). (1995). *Taking flight: My story by Vicki Van Meter.* New York: Viking.

Williams, S. R. (1976). *Demeter's daughters: The women who founded America 1587–1787.* New York: Atheneum.

Xong, B. (1989). *Nine in one Grr! Grr! A folktale from the Hmong people of Laos.* Emeryville, CA: Children's Book Press.

Websites

The National Women's History Project website at **www.nwhp.org/progidea.html** provides extensive information, resources, and ideas for teaching about women's history.

Information about the 150th anniversary of the U.S. women's rights movement can be found at **www.Legacy98.org**.

 **Spring**

Language and Literacy Experiences

Observing and Writing about Experiences

- *Planting:* Children plant bean seeds (soaked in water first) in plastic tumblers or flower or grass seeds or bedding plants in pots, window boxes, or patches of earth.
- *Hatching:* Locate eggs and kits for the classroom (e.g., chickens, ducks, butterflies). Children keep observation journals of the progress of growing and hatching things, making drawings, labels, captions, measurements, graphs, and diagrams.

Poetry Walk and Journals

- *Poetry Walk:* Children take a walk on the schoolgrounds or in the neighborhood during spring and stop at intervals to write in poetry journals about sights, sounds, smells, feelings, images, similes, and metaphors.
- *Poetry Journals:* Use poetry journals as sources of ideas for children writing spring poetry and songs.
- *Read: In a Spring Garden* (Lewis, 1989).

Puppets and Props

- *Read:* Read picture books about animals, insects, and plants in spring, such as *Make Way for Ducklings* (McCloskey, 1941) and *The Very Hungry Caterpillar* (Carle, 1969).
- *Making Puppets and Props:* Students make puppets and props of the characters from the book to retell or dramatize the story: for example, ducks (paper bag puppets with orange construction paper beaks), caterpillars (egg cartons split in half, painted, with pipe cleaner attenaes), and butterflies (butcher paper cutouts [one each front and back], painted, stapled and stuffed with newspaper).

Story Dramatizations

- *Stories: The Carrot Seed* (Krauss, 1945); *The Great Big Enormous Turnip* (Tolstoy, 1968); and *The Little Red Hen* (Galdone, 1973).

Photograms

- *Making Photograms:* Place small spring objects like seeds, leaves, and flowers on light-sensitive paper and expose to sunlight for a few minutes; rinse the paper in water and see the impression made by the object.
- *Read: A, B, See!* (Hoban, 1982), which is illustrated with photograms.

Lesson Plan: *Haiku*

Level: All grades

Purpose: Write about nature in the poetic form of haiku.

Teaching Sequence:

1. Read and discuss haiku, a Japanese form of nature poetry. A haiku follows the pattern of having 17 syllables in three lines (5–7–5). For an example, read *In a Spring Garden* (Lewis, 1989).
2. Bring spring flowers to class, such as daffodils, hyacinths, and crocuses. Ask the children to describe how each flower looks, smells, and feels, and record their observations on large Post-it notes. In addition to single words, encourage children to develop similes and metaphors about the flowers (e.g., *yellow as the sun*).
3. Create a chart with the headings "One-Syllable Words," "Two-Syllable Words," and "Three-Syllable Words." Then go through the Post-it notes and sort them by the number of syllables in each word or phrase. Position each note under the correct heading.
4. Using words and images from the chart, write a class haiku using this pattern:

   Haiku
   Line 1: 5 syllables
   Line 2: 7 syllables
   Line 3: 5 syllables

5. Ask children to write their own haiku about nature, taking ideas from plants and seeds grown in the classroom or something they saw or found on a nature walk, in a park, or in a home or public garden.

Extending Activities:

1. Read haiku aloud to children: *Black Swan/White Crow* (Lewis, 1995); *In the Eyes of the Cat: Japanese Poetry for all Seasons* (Demi, 1992); and *Cool Melons—Turn to Frogs! The Life and Poems of Issa* (Gollub, 1998).
2. As a class, visit a local Japanese garden or another type of public garden. Have students observe the setting and add images to their poetry journals.
3. Make a class collection of haiku and bind them together as a book, or display haiku on a bulletin board with illustrations in the Japanese style of art.

Lesson Plan: *Sing and Dance a Spring Song**

Level: Primary through upper grades

Purpose: Compose poetry, songs, and dances based on experiences in spring.

Teaching Sequence:

1. Do a class "word wall" of children's observations, associations, and images of spring, based on classroom or outdoor spring experiences (described earlier, e.g., planting, hatching, poetry walk): "IMAGES OF SPRING."
2. Use a familiar tune like "Frere Jacques" and count the number of syllables in each line. Fill in a chart organized according to the number of syllables per line with phrases from the word wall that have the same numbers of syllables:

*Thanks to Paul Boyd-Batstone for this idea.

"Spring Song" (to the tune of "Frere Jacques")

Line 1: 4 syllables _____

Line 2: 4 syllables _____

Line 3: 3 syllables _____

Line 4: 3 syllables _____

Line 5: 6 syllables _____

Line 6: 6 syllables _____

Line 7: 3 syllables _____

Line 8: 3 syllables _____

3. Sing the song together.
4. Add simple movements to each line that have the same number of syllables (e.g., waving arms in air, turning around with arms outstreched). Dance and sing the song. Add simple rhythm instruments: bells, tambourines, maracas, sandpaper blocks, rattles (e.g., dried beans inside two paper plates stapled together).

Extending Activities:

1. Create individual song sheets so children can write their own songs and create their own dances, or have children work in small groups.
2. Add props to dances, such as scarves, lengths of nylon net, and ribbon sticks (e.g., attach colorful ribbons to the end of a piece of dowel or an empty paper towel tube).
3. Plan a program for children to sing and dance their songs for other classes or parents. Make posters, programs, and ads for the school bulletin.
4. Make illustrated books of songs written by individuals or small groups.
5. Other tunes for songwriting: "Somewhere Over the Rainbow," "Row, Row, Row Your Boat," and "Old MacDonald Had a Farm."
6. Music for spring dancing songs: Grieg's "Little Bird"; "Papillon" ("Butterfly"), and "To Spring"; Respighi's "The Birds"; Rimsky-Korsakov's "Flight of the Bumble Bee"; Beethoven's Sonata no. 5 for Violin and Piano ("Spring") and Symphony no. 6 ("Pastoral"); Mendelssohn's Melody in F ("Spring Song"); and Vivaldi's "Spring" from "The Four Seasons."

Children's Books

Arnosky, J. (1987). *Sketching outdoors in spring.* New York: Lothrop, Lee & Shepard.

Carle, E. (1969). *The very hungry caterpillar.* New York: Philomel.

Demi (Ed.). (1992). *In the eyes of the cat: Japanese poetry for all seasons.* New York: Holt.

Galdone, P. (1973). *The little red hen.* New York: Clarion.

Gibbons, G. (1989). *Monarch butterfly.* New York: Holiday House.

Gibbons, G. (1991). *From seed to plant.* New York: Holiday House.

Gollub, M. (1998). *Cool melons—turn to frogs! The life and poems of Issa.* New York: Lee & Low.

Hirschi, R. (1990). *Spring.* New York: Dutton.

Hoban, T. (1982). *A, B, See!* New York: Greenwillow.

Horton, B. (1991). *What comes in spring?* New York: Knopf.

Krauss, R. (1945). *The carrot seed.* New York: Harper & Row.

Lauber, P. (1991). *Seeds: Pop-stick-glide.* New York: Crown.

Lewington, A. (1997). *Atlas of the rainforests.* Austin, TX: Raintree Steck–Vaughn.

Lewis, J. P. (1995). *Black swan/white crow.* New York: Atheneum.

Lewis, R. (1989). *In a spring garden.* New York: Dial.

McCloskey, R. (1941). *Make way for ducklings.* New York: Viking.

Rockwell, A. (1985). *First comes spring.* New York: Crowell.
Rockwell, A. (1998). *One bean.* New York: Rockwell.
Rucki, A. (1998). *When the earth wakes.* New York: Scholastic.
Tolstoy, A. (1968). *The great big enormous turnip.* New York: Watts.

Websites

Find ideas for garden-based learning from these sources:

National Gardening Association at **www.garden.org/edu** and **www.kidsgardening.com**

International Association of Japanese Gardens at **www.japanese-gardens-assoc.org**

Also go to **gardendigest.com/haiku3.htm** for a website that has information on gardens and haiku.

May   **Ecology**

Language and Literacy Experiences

Brainstorm Research Questions

- *Read Aloud and Discuss:* The teacher reads aloud *The Lost Lake* (Say, 1989), about a Japanese American father and son who find their vacation destination overrun by too many people, and asks children to discuss it.
- *Questions:* List students' questions of concern about ecology (e.g., preserving the environment, endangered animal species) and how to take action.

Reading for Information

- *Small Groups:* Children form groups around questions and read to answer them: *Fifty Simple Things You Can Do to Save the Earth* (Earthworks Group, 1991) and *The Big Book for Our Planet* (Durrell, George, & Paterson, 1994).

Letter Writing

- *Write for Information:* Children write to the Sierra Club (730 Polk St., San Francisco, CA 94109) or the National Wildlife Federation (1400 16th St. N.W., Washington, DC 20036).
- *Write to Take Action:* Contact local, state, and U.S. representatives (Conservation International, 1915 18th St. N.W., Washington, DC 20036).

Photo Essays

- *Creating Photo Essays:* Children photograph problems in the local environment and create photo essays, adding titles, captions, and actions to be taken.
- *Read Photoillustrated Books: Saving the Peregrine Falcon* (Arnold, 1985) and *Where Do Birds Live?* (Hirschi, 1987).

Lesson Plan: *How to Make the World More Beautiful*

Level: Primary through upper elementary grades

Purpose: Read, think, write, and take action.

Teaching Sequence:

1. Read aloud and discuss *Miss Rumphius* (Cooney, 1982), about a woman who tries to make the world a more beautiful place. Ask children these questions:

    What did you think of the book?

    How could you make the world a more beautiful place?

2. Create a class list of children's ideas for beautifying the world, and continue to add to it as new ideas come up. Suggest that children talk to their families, read the newspaper, and watch television news programs for new ideas.

3. Have each child choose one thing that he or she could do to make the world more beautiful. Encourage students to give their selections some serious thought and then write about how they could accomplish these tasks.

4. Ask children to share their ideas, and discuss them as a class. Together, decide on one thing to do as a class, such as be responsible for picking up trash on a regular basis, plant flowers on the schoolgrounds, or paint a mural in the community.

5. As a class, brainstorm ideas for completing the project and make a plan to take action. Form groups, as needed, to research different aspects of the project or to complete separate steps. For instance, if the project were to plant flowers, small groups of students could be assigned to these separate tasks: write a letter to the principal about doing so and find out what kinds of flowers would grow well, how much they would cost, where to get seeds or plants, what gardening tools would be needed, and what time frame should be followed to put the plan into action.

6. Put the plan into action. Document everything students do by keeping a class journal, photographing or videotaping events, and audiotaping commentaries and interviews. Publicize what students have done using a bulletin board of photos and captions arranged along a timeline, a video documentary, an article in the school district or PTA newsletter, or a letter to the editor of the local newspaper.

Extending Activities:

1. Read aloud other books about people who have tried to make the world more beautiful, such as *Johnny Appleseed* (Kellogg, 1988) (see Chapter 4). Discuss and then compare and contrast the book with *Miss Rumphius* (Cooney, 1982) using a Venn diagram.

2. Have students write memos or letters to other classes and schools in which they offer to speak to their peers about taking action.

3. Look at websites for ideas about a class or school garden, including the following:

    National Gardening Association at **www.garden.org/edu and www. kidsgardening.com**

    International Association of Japanese Gardens **at www.japanese-gardens-assoc.org**

    Garden Digest at **gardendigest.com**

Lesson Plan: *Story Dramatization of*
The Great Kapok Tree, *by Lynne Cherry*

Level: Primary through upper grades

Purpose: Read, discuss, and dramatize a story with an ecology theme.

Teaching Sequence:
1. Read aloud *The Great Kapok Tree* (Cherry, 1990), a picture book about the animals, plants, and Yanomamo people of the Amazon rainforest and what could happen if it were destroyed. Discuss with children, asking: "What did you think of the story?" "What was your favorite part?" "What do you think will happen to the rainforest?"
2. Plan a story dramatization based on the book. Make a chart, and fill in as students continue to discuss the story and how to dramatize it:

The Great Kapok Tree

Setting: Amazon rainforest, around large kapok tree

Characters: Narrator, boss, woodcutter, Yanomamo child, rainforest animals (boa constrictor, bees and butterflies, monkeys, birds [toucan, macaw, cock-of-the-rock], frogs, jaguar, tree porcupines, and sloth).

Plot:
(1) Boss tells woodcutter to chop down tree.
(2) Woodcutter starts to chop down tree but falls asleep.
(3) Animals tell him why he shouldn't chop down tree.
(4) Woodcutter wakes up and leaves without chopping down tree.

3. Cast the characters and make a large space for playing the story.
4. Play the story: The narrator (student or teacher) reads the narrative part of text aloud, and the characters speak their parts to the sleeping man. Play the story several times, so children can play different characters.
5. Ask students how they felt about playing the story, what they liked about how different children acted out the characters and plot, and what they might do next time to make it better.

Extending Activities:
1. To produce a musical of the book, use the cassette tape *The Great Kapok Tree* (music by Paul Boyd-Batstone), which has lyrics for 12 songs based on the book and a teacher's guide with a rainforest unit, music, ideas for staging the book as a musical, making props, and a bibliography of resources. (Order it from Dr. Paul Boyd-Batstone, 5106 E. El Roble St., Long Beach, CA 90815-1139.)
2. Read *One Day in a Tropical Rainforest* (George, 1990); *Rain Forest Secrets* (Dorros, 1990); *Nature's Green Umbrella: Tropical Rain Forests* (Gibbons, 1994;) *Make Your Own Rainforest* (Johnston, 1993); *Welcome to the Green House* (Yolen, 1993); and *Fernando's Gift* (Keister, 1997).
3. For information or advocacy about protecting the rainforests, write letters to Children's Rainforest (P.O. Box 936, Lewiston, ME 04240) and Rainforest Action Network (450 Sansome, Suite 700, San Francisco, CA 94111).

Children's Books

Azimov, I. (1992). *Why are the rainforests vanishing?* Milwaukee, WI: Gareth Stevens.
Cherry, L. (1990). *The great Kapok tree.* New York: HarBrace.
Cherry, L., & Plotkin, M. J. (1998). *The shaman's apprentice: A tale of the Amazon rain forest.* San Diego: Harcourt Brace Jovanovich.
Chinery, M. (1992). *Rainforest animals.* New York: Random House.

Cooney, B. (1982). *Miss Rumphius.* New York: Penguin.

Dorros A. (1990). *Rain forest secrets.* New York: Scholastic.

Durrell, A., George, J., & Paterson, K. (Eds.). (1994). *The big book for our planet.* New York: Dutton.

Earthworks Group. (1991). *Fifty simple things you can do to save the earth.* Kansas City, KS: Earthworks.

George, J. (1990). *One day in a tropical rainforest.* New York: Crowell.

Gibbons, G. (1994). *Nature's green umbrella: Tropical rain forests.* New York: Morrow.

Hirschi, R. (1987). *Where do birds live?* New York: Walker.

Holmes, A. (1993). *I can save the earth: A kid's handbook for keeping earth healthy and green.* New York: Julian Messner.

Hughes, T. (1995). *The iron woman.* New York: Dial.

Jeffers, S. (1991). *Brother Eagle, Sister Sky: A message from Chief Seattle.* New York: Dial.

Johnston, D. (1993). *Make your own rainforest.* New York: Lodestar.

Jonas, A. (1990). *Aardvarks disembark.* New York: Greenwillow.

Keister, D. (1997). *Fernando's gift/El regalo de Fernando.* New York: Little, Brown.

Kellogg, S. (1988). *Johnny Appleseed.* New York: Morrow.

Lauber, P. (1988). *Summer of fire: Yellowstone, 1988.* New York: Orchard.

Say, A. (1989). *The lost lake.* Boston: Houghton Mifflin.

Seuss, Dr. (1981). *The lorax.* New York: Random House.

Yolen, J. (1993). *Welcome to the green house.* New York: Putnam's.

Websites

Find information, resources, and teaching activities about the rainforest at **www.rainforest-alliance.org/**, and download teaching packets on environmental education from the National Wildlife Federation at **nwf.org/nwf/**.

Consult these websites for information on gardens and gardening:

National Gardening Association at **www.garden.org/edu** and **www.kidsgardening.com**

International Association of Japanese Gardens at **www.japanese-gardens-assoc.org**

Garden Digest at **gardendigest.com**

 The Future

Language and Literacy Experiences

Picture the Future

■ *Read and Discuss:* The teacher reads aloud *Just a Dream* (Van Allsburg, 1990) and asks students to discuss it.

■ *Drawing and Writing:* Students draw pictures of and write about what the future might be like.

Reading and Writing Future Fiction

■ *Read Aloud:* The teacher reads aloud *The Green Book* (Paton, 1982), for younger students, or *The Giver* (Lowry, 1993), for older ones.

■ *Write:* Children write stories about what life in the future might be like.

Future Filmmaking
- *Scriptwriting:* Students develop scripts for filmmaking based on reading and writing future fiction.
- *Producing:* Children make videotaped films, filmstrips, or computer displays with hyperstudio.

Local History Project
- *Changes over the Years:* Students learn how their town has changed by interviewing people who have lived in the area for a long time, finding photographs of the area taken over time, and reading accounts of what it used to be like (e.g., in old newspapers, magazines).
- *Changes to Come:* Children make predictions about what the area will be like in the future, based on how it has changed in the past. Invite a city council person or official to talk to the class.
- *Mural:* The class makes a mural—"Our Town: Past, Present, and Future"—displaying what they've learned.
- *Read: Where the Forest Meets the Sea* (Baker, 1987); *Window* (Baker, 1991); *The Little House* (Burton, 1942); *Story of an English Village* (Goodall, 1989); *New Providence: A Changing City Scape* (Von Tscharner & Fleming, 1987); *Toddlecreek Post Office* (Shulevitz, 1990); *The Changing Countryside* (Muller, 1977b); *The Changing City* (Muller, 1977a); *Shaker Lane* (Provensen & Provensen, 1988); *My Place* (Wheatley, 1990); and *Heron Street* (Turner, 1989).
- *Write:* Students write memoirs as though they lived in an earlier time.

Lesson Plan: *Future World Theme Park*

Level: Primary through upper grades

Purpose: Imagine, draw, write, and construct a model of Future World Theme Park.

Teaching Sequence:
1. After a period of thinking, talking, reading, and writing about the future, make plans for Future World Theme Park, to be constructed in the classroom. Brainstorm ideas and record on chartpaper for "What Future World Would Be Like" and "How to Create Future World."
2. Categorize ideas and form groups to make plans for creating Future World, such as signs and murals, maps, models and dioramas, exhibits, computer demonstrations, and interactive displays (e.g., hyperstudio, videos, photo essays, live shows and dramatizations, and rides).
3. Each group makes (a) a diagram of what they want to construct, with a written explanation of how they will do it, (b) a time frame for doing it, and (c) a list of materials they will need.
4. Groups report to the class what they will do and record ideas on a "wall chart" as a plan for building Future World.

Extending Activities:
1. Over a 2- to 3-week period, groups carry out their plans to turn the classroom into Future World, continuing to read, discuss, write, plan, and construct parts of it.

2. Invite other classes and parents to visit Future World: make posters advertising its opening, write announcements for the school bulletin and electronic bulletin boards, videotape a commercial to show in other classrooms, and make tickets and free passes.
3. Invite the local newspaper to visit and report on Future World.
4. Take pictures for a book students will write: *How We Made Future World.*
5. Use Sim City software to create a future simulation.

Lesson Plan: *Time Capsule*

Level: Primary through middle school grades

Purpose: Develop skills in critical thinking, research, and expository reading and writing.

Teaching Sequence:
1. Have students brainstorm a list of things to include in a time capsule that would show children in the future what the world is like today.
2. Form groups and assign them items to collect: newspapers and magazines, artifacts such as commercial products, a picture of the school and class, and so on.
3. As a class, create a "word wall" of ideas about what the world is like today, what students think it will be like in the future, and what they hope it will be like in the future.
4. Using the word wall as a model, have students write their own messages to the children of the future. Then ask students to illustrate their messages and attach pictures of themselves.
5. As a class, write a language experience story explaining the time capsule project.
6. Put the class story, the artifacts, and the student messages and illustrations in a metal box and bury it on the schoolgrounds.

Extending Activities:
1. Help children make a bulletin board display of this project, including a list and photos of the things in the time capsule, copies of their individual messages, a written explanation of the project, and photos of the children preparing and burying the capsule.
2. Have students interview parents or grandparents to find out what the world was like when they were children. They should ask questions such as these:
   What did they play with? wear? eat?
   What did they do in school?
   Who was president?
   What historical events characterized the era?
   Also have students ask their subjects about what they thought the world would be like in the future. Are they surprised or maybe even disappointed?

Children's Books

Alcock, V. (1988). *The monster garden.* New York: Delacorte.
Baker, J. (1987). *Where the forest meets the sea.* New York: Greenwillow.
Baker, J. (1991). *Window.* New York: Greenwillow.
Bunting, E. (1990). *Fly away home.* New York: Clarion.

Burton, V. L. (1942). *The little house.* Boston: Houghton Mifflin.
Christopher, J. (1967a). *The city of gold and lead.* New York: Macmillan.
Christopher, J. (1967b). *The White Mountains.* New York: Macmillan.
Christopher, J. (1988). *When the tripods came.* New York: Dutton.
Dickenson, P. (1989). *Eva.* New York: Delacorte.
Durrell, A., & Sachs, M. (1990). *The big book for peace.* New York: Dutton.
Goodall, J. (1989). *Story of an English village.* New York: McElderry.
Lowry, L. (1993). *The giver.* Boston: Houghton Mifflin.
MacDonald, C. (1989). *The lake at the end of the world.* New York: Dial.
Muller, J. (1977a). *The changing city.* New York: Atheneum.
Muller, J. (1977b). *The changing countryside.* New York: Atheneum.
O'Brien, R. (1975). *Z for Zachariah.* New York: Atheneum.
Paton, J. (1982). *The green book.* New York: Farrar, Straus, & Giroux.
Provensen, A., & Provensen, M. (1988). *Shaker Lane.* New York: Penguin.
Shulevitz, U. (1990). *Toddlecreek Post Office.* New York: Farrar, Straus, & Giroux.
Turner, A. (1989). *Heron Street.* New York: Harper & Row.
Van Allsburg, C. (1990). *Just a dream.* Boston: Houghton Mifflin.
Von Tscharner, R., & Fleming, R. (1987). *New Providence: A changing city scape.* New York: Harcourt Brace Jovanovich.
Wheatley, N. (1990). *My place.* Melbourne, Australia: Australia in Print.

Websites

The future is here at **www.starport.com/places/forKids**, a compendium of links to sites and pages on the World Wide Web that are interesting to children. See **www.the-childrens-society.org.uk/information/plan_env_feb98/case_study. html** for how to do local history projects and involve children in real local community or environmental planning projects.

John Newbery Medal

The John Newbery Medal has been awarded annually since 1922 under the supervision of the Association for Library Service to Children of the American Library Association. It is presented to the author of the most distinguished contribution to literature for children published in the United States during the previous year. One or more Honor Books are also chosen. Winners must be residents or citizens of the United States.

1922
The Story of Mankind by Hendrik Willem van
    Loon (Liveright)
Honor Books
Cedric the Forester by Bernard Marshall (Appleton)
The Golden Fleece and the Heroes Who Lived before
    Achilles by Padraic Colum (Macmillan)
The Great Quest by Charles Hawes (Little, Brown)
The Old Tobacco Shop by William Bowen
    (Macmillan)
Windy Hill by Cornelia Meigs (Macmillan)

1923
The Voyages of Doctor Dolittle by Hugh Lofting
    (Lippincott)
Honor Book
No record

1924
The Dark Frigate by Charles Hawes (Atlantic/
    Little, Brown)
Honor Book
No record

1925
Tales from Silver Lands by Charles Finger
   (Doubleday)
Honor Books
Dream Coach by Anne Parrish (Macmillan)
Nicholas by Anne Carroll Moore (Putnam)
1926
Shen of the Sea by Arthur Bowie Chrisman (Dutton)
Honor Book
Voyagers by Padraic Colum (Macmillan)
1927
Smoky, the Cowhorse by Will James (Scribner's)
Honor Book
No record
1928
Gayneck, the Story of a Pigeon by Dhan Gopal
   Mukerji (Dutton)
Honor Books
Downright Dencey by Caroline Snedeker
   (Doubleday)
The Wonder Smith and His Son by Ella Young
   (Longmans)
1929
The Trumpeter of Krakow by Eric P. Kelly
   (Macmillan)
Honor Books
The Boy Who Was by Grace Hallock (Dutton)
Clearing Weather by Cornelia Meigs (Little, Brown)
Millions of Cats by Wanda Gág (Coward)
Pigtail of Ah Lee Ben Loo by John Bennett
   (Longmans)
Runaway Papoose by Grace Moon (Doubleday)
Tod of the Fens by Elinor Whitney (Macmillan)
1930
Hitty, Her First Hundred Years by Rachel Field
   (Macmillan)
Honor Books
Daughter of the Seine by Jeanette Eaton (Harper)
Jumping-Off Place by Marian Hurd McNeely
   (Longmans)
Little Blacknose by Hildegarde Swift (Harcourt)
Pran of Albania by Elizabeth Miller (Doubleday)
Tangle-Coated Horse and Other Tales by Ella Young
   (Longmans)
Vaino by Julia Davis Adams (Dutton)
1931
The Cat Who Went to Heaven by Elizabeth
   Coatsworth (Macmillan)
Honor Books
The Dark Star of Itza by Alida Malkus (Harcourt)
Floating Island by Anne Parrish (Harper)
Garram the Hunter by Herbert Best (Doubleday)
Meggy Macintosh by Elizabeth Janet Gray
   (Doubleday)
Mountains Are Free by Julia Davis Adams (Dutton)
Ood-Le-Uk the Wanderer by Alice Lide and
   Margaret Johansen (Little, Brown)
Queer Person by Ralph Hubbard (Doubleday)
Spice and the Devil's Cake by Agnes Hewes (Knopf)

1932
Waterless Mountain by Laura Adams Armer
   (Longmans)
Honor Books
Boy of the South Seas by Eunice Tietjens (Coward)
Calico Bush by Rachel Field (Macmillan)
The Fairy Circus by Dorothy P. Lathrop
   (Macmillan)
Jane's Island by Marjorie Allee (Houghton Mifflin)
Out of the Flames by Eloise Lownsbery (Longmans)
Truce of the Wolf and Other Tales of Old Italy by
   Mary Gould Davis (Harcourt)
1933
Young Fu of the Upper Yangtze by Elizabeth Lewis
   (Winston)
Honor Books
Children of the Soil by Nora Burglon (Doubleday)
The Railroad to Freedom by Hildegarde Swift
   (Harcourt)
Swift Rivers by Cornelia Meigs (Little, Brown)
1934
Invincible Louisa by Cornelia Meigs (Little, Brown)
Honor Books
ABC Bunny by Wanda Gág (Coward)
Apprentice of Florence by Anne Kyle (Houghton
   Mifflin)
Big Tree of Bunlahy by Padraic Colum (Macmillan)
The Forgotten Daughter by Caroline Snedeker
   (Doubleday)
Glory of the Seas by Agnes Hewes (Knopf)
New Land by Sarah Schmidt (McBride)
Swords of Steel by Elsie Singmaster (Houghton
   Mifflin)
Winged Girl of Knossos by Erik Berry (Appleton)
1935
Dobry by Monica Shannon (Viking)
Honor Books
Davy Crockett by Constance Rourke (Harcourt)
Day on Skates by Hilda Van Stockum (Harper)
Pageant of Chinese History by Elizabeth Seeger
   (Longmans)
1936
Caddie Woodlawn by Carol Ryrie Brink
   (Macmillan)
Honor Books
All Sail Set by Armstrong Sperry (Winston)
The Good Master by Kate Seredy (Viking)
Honk, the Moose by Phil Strong (Dodd)
Young Walter Scott by Elizabeth Janet Gray
   (Viking)
1937
Roller Skates by Ruth Sawyer (Viking)
Honor Books
Audubon by Constance Rourke (Harcourt)
The Codfish Musket by Agnes Hewes (Doubleday)
Golden Basket by Ludwig Bemelmans (Viking)
Phebe Fairchild: Her Book by Lois Lenski (Stokes)
Whistler's Van by Idwal Jones (Viking)
Winterbound by Margery Bianco (Viking)

1938
The White Stag by Kate Seredy (Viking)
Honor Books
Bright Island by Mabel Robinson (Random House)
On the Banks of Plum Creek by Laura Ingalls Wilder
(Harper)
Pecos Bill by James Cloyd Bowman (Little, Brown)

1939
Thimble Summer by Elizabeth Enright (Rinehart)
Honor Books
Hello the Boat! by Phyllis Crawford (Holt)
*Leader by Destiny: George Washington, Man and
Patriot* by Jeanette Eaton (Harcourt)
Mr. Popper's Penguins by Richard and Florence
Atwater (Little, Brown)
Nino by Valenti Angelo (Viking)
Penn by Elizabeth Janet Gray (Viking)

1940
Daniel Boone by James Daugherty (Viking)
Honor Books
Boy with a Pack by Stephen W. Meader (Harcourt)
By the Shores of Silver Lake by Laura Ingalls Wilder
(Harper)
Runner of the Mountain Tops by Mabel Robinson
(Random House)
The Singing Tree by Kate Seredy (Viking)

1941
Call It Courage by Armstrong Sperry (Macmillan)
Honor Books
Blue Willow by Doris Gates (Viking)
The Long Winter by Laura Ingalls Wilder (Harper)
Nansen by Anna Gertrude Hall (Viking)
Young Mac of Fort Vancouver by Mary Jane Carr
(Crowell)

1942
The Matchlock Gun by Walter D. Edmonds (Dodd)
Honor Books
Down Ryton Water by Eva Roe Gaggin (Viking)
George Washington's World by Genevieve Foster
(Scribner's)
Indian Captive: The Story of Mary Jemison by Lois
Lenski (Lippincott)
Little Town on the Prairie by Laura Ingalls Wilder
(Harper)

1943
Adam of the Road by Elizabeth Janet Gray (Viking)
Honor Books
Have You Seen Tom Thumb? by Mabel Leigh Hunt
(Lippincott)
The Middle Moffat by Eleanor Estes (Harcourt)

1944
Johnny Tremain by Esther Forbes (Houghton
Mifflin)
Honor Books
Fog Magic by Julia Sauer (Viking)
Mountain Born by Elizabeth Yates (Coward)
Rufus M. by Eleanor Estes (Harcourt)
These Happy Golden Years by Laura Ingalls Wilder
(Harper)

1945
Rabbit Hill by Robert Lawson (Viking)
Honor Books
Abraham Lincoln's World by Genevieve Foster
(Scribner's)
The Hundred Dresses by Eleanor Estes (Harcourt)
Lone Journey: The Life of Roger Williams by Jeanette
Eaton (Harcourt)
The Silver Pencil by Alice Dalgliesh (Scribner's)

1946
Strawberry Girl by Lois Lenski (Lippincott)
Honor Books
Bhimsa, the Dancing Bear by Christine Weston
(Scribner's)
Justin Morgan Had a Horse by Marguerite Henry
(Rand McNally)
The Moved-Outers by Florence Crannell Means
(Houghton Mifflin)
New Found World by Katherine Shippen (Viking)

1947
Miss Hickory by Carolyn Sherwin Bailey (Viking)
Honor Books
The Avion My Uncle Flew by Cyrus Fisher
(Appleton)
Big Tree by Mary and Conrad Buff (Viking)
The Heavenly Tenants by William Maxwell
(Harper)
The Hidden Treasure of Glaston by Eleanore Jewett
(Viking)
Wonderful Year by Nancy Barnes (Messner)

1948
The Twenty-One Balloons by William Pène du Bois
(Viking)
Honor Books
The Cow-Tail Switch and Other West African Stories
by Harold Courlander (Holt)
Li Lun, Lad of Courage by Carolyn Treffinger
(Abingdon)
Misty of Chincoteague by Marguerite Henry (Rand
McNally)
Pancakes—Paris by Claire Huchet Bishop (Viking)
The Quaint and Curious Quest of Johnny Longfoot by
Catherine Besterman (Bobbs)

1949
King of the Wind by Marguerite Henry (Rand
McNally)
Honor Books
Daughter of the Mountains by Louise Rankin
(Viking)
My Father's Dragon by Ruth S. Gannett (Random
House)
Seabird by Holling C. Holling (Houghton Mifflin)
Story of the Negro by Arna Bontemps (Knopf)

1950
A Door in the Wall by Marguerite de Angeli
(Doubleday)
Honor Books
The Blue Cat of Castle Town by Catherine Coblentz
(Longmans)

George Washington by Genevieve Foster (Scribner's)
Kildee House by Rutherford Montgomery
    (Doubleday)
Song of the Pines by Walter and Marion Havighurst
    (Winston)
Tree of Freedom by Rebecca Caudill (Viking)
1951
Amos Fortune, Free Man by Elizabeth Yates (Dutton)
Honor Books
Abraham Lincoln, Friend of the People by Clara
    Ingram Judson (Follett)
Better Known as Johnny Appleseed by Mabel Leigh
    Hunt (Lippincott)
Gandhi, Fighter without a Sword by Jeanette Eaton
    (Morrow)
The Story of Appleby Capple by Anne Parrish
    (Harper)
1952
Ginger Pye by Eleanor Estes (Harcourt)
Honor Books
Americans before Columbus by Elizabeth Baity
    (Viking)
The Apple and the Arrow by Mary and Conrad Buff
    (Houghton Mifflin)
The Defender by Nicholas Kalashnikoff (Scribner's)
The Light at Tern Rocks by Julia Sauer (Viking)
Minn of the Mississippi by Holling C. Holling
    (Houghton Mifflin)
1953
Secret of the Andes by Ann Nolan Clark (Viking)
Honor Books
The Bears of Hemlock Mountain by Alice Dalgliesh
    (Scribner's)
Birthdays of Freedom, Vol. 1 by Genevieve Foster
    (Scribner's)
Charlotte's Web by E. B. White (Harper)
Moccasin Trail by Eloise McGraw (Coward)
Red Sails to Capri by Ann Weil (Viking)
1954
. . . *And Now Miguel* by Joseph Krumgold (Crowell)
Honor Books
All Alone by Claire Huchet Bishop (Viking)
Hurry Home Candy by Meindert DeJong (Harper)
Magic Maize by Mary and Conrad Buff (Houghton
    Mifflin)
Shadrach by Meindert DeJong (Harper)
Theodore Roosevelt, Fighting Patriot by Clara Ingram
    Judson (Follett)
1955
The Wheel on the School by Meindert DeJong
    (Harper)
Honor Books
Banner in the Sky by James Ullman (Lippincott)
Courage of Sarah Noble by Alice Dalgliesh
    (Scribner's)
1956
Carry On, Mr. Bowditch by Jean Lee Latham
    (Houghton Mifflin)

Honor Books
The Golden Name Day by Jennie Lindquist
    (Harper)
Men, Microscopes, and Living Things by Katherine
    Shippen (Viking)
The Secret River by Marjorie Kinnan Rawlings
    (Scribner's)
1957
Miracles on Maple Hill by Virginia Sorensen
    (Harcourt)
Honor Books
Black Fox of Lorne by Marguerite de Angeli (Doubleday)
The Corn Grows Ripe by Dorothy Rhoads (Viking)
The House of Sixty Fathers by Meindert DeJong
    (Harper)
Mr. Justice Holmes by Clara Ingram Judson (Follett)
Old Yeller by Fred Gipson (Harper)
1958
Rifles for Watie by Harold Keith (Crowell)
Honor Books
Gone-Away Lake by Elizabeth Enright (Harcourt)
The Great Wheel by Robert Lawson (Viking)
The Horse Catcher by Mari Sandoz (Westminster)
Tom Paine, Freedom's Apostle by Leo Gurko
    (Crowell)
1959
The Witch of Blackbird Pond by Elizabeth George
    Speare (Houghton Mifflin)
Honor Books
Along Came a Dog by Meindert DeJong (Harper)
Chucaro: Wild Pony of the Pampa by Francis Kalnay
    (Harcourt)
The Family under the Bridge by Natalie Savage
    Carlson (Harper)
The Perilous Road by William O. Steele (Harcourt)
1960
Onion John by Joseph Krumgold (Crowell)
Honor Books
America Is Born by Gerald W. Johnson (Morrow)
The Gammage Cup by Carol Kendall (Harcourt)
My Side of the Mountain by Jean Craighead George
    (Dutton)
1961
Island of the Blue Dolphins by Scott O'Dell
    (Houghton Mifflin)
Honor Books
America Moves Forward by Gerald W. Johnson
    (Morrow)
The Cricket in Times Square by George Selden
    (Farrar)
Old Ramon by Jack Schaefer (Houghton Mifflin)
1962
The Bronze Bow by Elizabeth George Speare
    (Houghton Mifflin)
Honor Books
Belling the Tiger by Mary Stolz (Harper)
Frontier Living by Edwin Tunis (World)
The Golden Goblet by Eloise McGraw (Coward)

1963
A Wrinkle in Time by Madeleine L'Engle (Farrar)
Honor Books
Men of Athens by Olivia Coolidge (Houghton
  Mifflin)
Thistle and Thyme by Sorche Nic Leodhas (Holt)
1964
It's Like This, Cat by Emily Cheney Neville
  (Harper)
Honor Books
The Loner by Ester Wier (McKay)
Rascal by Sterling North (Dutton)
1965
Shadow of a Bull by Maia Wojciechowska
  (Atheneum)
Honor Books
Across Five Aprils by Irene Hunt (Follett)
1966
I, Juan de Pareja by Elizabeth Borten de Trevino
  (Farrar)
Honor Books
The Animal Family by Randall Jarrell (Pantheon)
The Black Cauldron by Lloyd Alexander (Holt)
The Noonday Friends by Mary Stolz (Harper)
1967
Up a Road Slowly by Irene Hunt (Follett)
Honor Books
The Jazz Man by Mary H. Weik (Atheneum)
The King's Fifth by Scott O'Dell (Houghton)
Zlateh the Goat and Other Stories by Isaac Bashevis
  Singer (Harper)
1968
From the Mixed-Up Files of Mrs. Basil E. Frankweiler
  by E. L. Konigsburg (Atheneum)
Honor Books
The Black Pearl by Scott O'Dell (Houghton
  Mifflin)
The Egypt Game by Zilpha Keatley Snyder
  (Atheneum)
The Fearsome Inn by Isaac Bashevis Singer
  (Scribner's)
*Jennifer, Hecate, Macbeth, William McKinley, and
  Me, Elizabeth* by E. L. Konigsburg (Atheneum)
1969
The High King by Lloyd Alexander (Holt)
Honor Books
To Be a Slave by Julius Lester (Dial)
When Sheemiel Went to Warsaw and Other Stories
  by Isaac Bashevis Singer (Farrar)
1970
Sounder by William H. Armstrong (Harper)
Honor Books
Journey Outside by Mary Q. Steele (Viking)
*The Many Ways of Seeing: An Introduction to the
  Pleasures of Art* by Janet Gaylord Moore
  (World)
Our Eddie by Sulamith Ish-Kishor (Pantheon)

1971
Summer of the Swans by Betsy Byars (Viking)
Honor Books
Enchantress from the Stars by Sylvia Louise Engdahl
  (Atheneum)
Knee-Knock Rise by Natalie Babbitt (Farrar)
Sing Down the Moon by Scott O'Dell (Houghton
  Mifflin)
1972
Mrs. Frisby and the Rats of NIMH by Robert C.
  O'Brien (Atheneum)
Honor Books
Annie and the Old One by Miska Miles
  (Atlantic/Little, Brown)
The Headless Cupid by Zilpha Keatley Snyder
  (Atheneum)
Incident at Hawk's Hill by Allan W. Eckert (Little,
  Brown)
The Planet of Junior Brown by Virginia Hamilton
  (Macmillan)
The Tombs of Atuan by Ursula K. Le Guin
  (Atheneum)
1973
Julie of the Wolves by Jean Craighead George
  (Harper)
Honor Books
Frog and Toad Together by Arnold Lobel (Harper)
The Upstairs Room by Johanna Reiss (Crowell)
The Witches of Worm by Zilpha Keatley Snyder
  (Atheneum)
1974
The Slave Dancer by Paula Fox (Bradbury)
Honor Book
The Dark Is Rising by Susan Cooper (McElderry)
1975
M. C. Higgins, the Great by Virginia Hamilton
  (Macmillan)
Honor Books
Figgs and Phantoms by Ellen Raskin (Dutton)
My Brother Sam Is Dead by James Lincoln Collier
  and Christopher Collier (Four Winds)
The Perilous Gard by Elizabeth Marie Pope
  (Houghton Mifflin)
Philip Hall Likes Me, I Reckon Maybe by Bette
  Greene (Dial)
1976
The Grey King by Susan Cooper (McElderry)
Honor Books
Dragonwings by Laurence Yep (Harper)
The Hundred Penny Box by Sharon Bell Mathis
  (Viking)
1977
Roll of Thunder, Hear My Cry by Mildred D. Taylor
  (Dial)
Honor Books
Abel's Island by William Steig (Farrar)
A String in the Harp by Nancy Bond (McElderry)

1978
Bridge to Terabithia by Katherine Paterson
  (Crowell)
Honor Books
Anpao: An American Indian Odyssey by Jamake
  Highwater (Lippincott)
Ramona and Her Father by Beverly Cleary (Morrow)
1979
The Westing Game by Ellen Raskin (Dutton)
Honor Books
The Great Gilly Hopkins by Katherine Paterson
  (Crowell)
1980
*A Gathering of Days: A New England Girl's Journal,
  1830–32* by Joan W. Blos (Scribner's)
Honor Book
The Road from Home: The Story of an Armenian Girl
  by David Kherdian (Greenwillow)
1981
Jacob Have I Loved by Katherine Paterson
  (Crowell)
Honor Books
The Fledgling by Jane Langton (Harper)
A Ring of Endless Light by Madeleine L'Engle
  (Farrar)
1982
*A Visit to William Blake's Inn: Poems for Innocent and
  Experienced Travelers* by Nancy Willard
  (Harcourt)
Honor Books
Ramona Quimby, Age 8 by Beverly Cleary (Morrow)
*Upon the Head of the Goat: A Childhood in Hungary,
  1939–1944* by Aranka Siegal (Farrar)
1983
Dicey's Song by Cynthia Voigt (Atheneum)
Honor Books
The Blue Sword by Robin McKinley (Greenwillow)
Doctor De Soto by William Steig (Farrar)
Graven Images by Paul Fleischman (Harper)
Homesick: My Own Story by Jean Fritz (Putnam)
Sweet Whispers, Brother Rush by Virginia Hamilton
  (Philomel)
1984
Dear Mr. Henshaw by Beverly Cleary (Morrow)
Honor Books
The Sign of the Beaver by Elizabeth George Speare
  (Houghton Mifflin)
A Solitary Blue by Cynthia Voigt (Atheneum)
Sugaring Time by Kathryn Lasky (Macmillan)
The Wish Giver by Bill Brittain (Harper)
1985
The Hero and the Crown by Robin McKinley
  (Greenwillow)
Honor Books
Like Jake and Me by Mavis Jukes (Knopf)
The Moves Make the Man by Bruce Brooks
  (Harper)
One-Eyed Cat by Paula Fox (Bradbury)

1986
Sarah, Plain and Tall by Patricia MacLachlan
  (Harper)
Honor Books
Commodore Perry in the Land of the Shogun by
  Rhoda Blumberg (Lothrop)
Dogsong by Gary Paulsen (Bradbury)
1987
The Whipping Boy by Sid Fleischman
  (Greenwillow)
Honor Books
A Fine White Dust by Cynthia Rylant
  (Bradbury)
On My Honor by Marion Dane Bauer (Clarion)
*Volcano: The Eruption and Healing of Mount St.
  Helens* by Patricia Lauber (Bradbury)
1988
Lincoln: A Photobiography by Russell Freedman
  (Clarion)
Honor Books
After the Rain by Norma Fox Mazer (Morrow)
Hatchet by Gary Paulsen (Bradbury)
1989
Joyful Noise: Poems for Two Voices by Paul
  Fleischman (Harper)
Honor Books
*In the Beginning: Creation Stories from Around the
  World* by Virginia Hamilton (Harcourt)
Scorpions by Walter Dean Myers (Harper)
1990
Number the Stars by Lois Lowry (Houghton
  Mifflin)
Honor Books
Afternoon of the Elves by Janet Taylor Lisle
  (Orchard)
Shabanu: Daughter of the Wind by Suzanne Fisher
  Staples (Knopf)
The Winter Room by Gary Paulsen (Orchard)
1991
Maniac Magee by Jerry Spinelli (Little, Brown)
Honor Book
The True Confessions of Charlotte Doyle by Avi
  (Orchard)
1992
Shiloh by Phyllis Reynolds Naylor (Atheneum)
Honor Books
Nothing but the Truth: A Documentary Novel by Avi
  (Orchard)
The Wright Brothers: How They Invented the Airplane
  by Russell Freedman (Holiday House)
1993
Missing May by Cynthia Rylant (Orchard)
Honor Books
The Dark-Thirty: Southern Tales of the Supernatural
  by Patricia McKissack (Knopf)
Somewhere in the Darkness by Walter Dean Myers
  (Scholastic)
What Hearts by Bruce Brooks (HarperCollins)

1994
The Giver by Lois Lowry (Houghton Mifflin)
Honor Books
Crazy Lady! by Jane Leslie Conly (HarperCollins)
Dragon's Gate by Laurence Yep (HarperCollins)
Eleanor Roosevelt: A Life of Discovery by Russell
    Freedman (Clarion)
1995
Walk Two Moons by Sharon Creech
    (HarperCollins)
Honor Books
Catherine, Called Birdy by Karen Cushman
    (Clarion)
The Ear, the Eye and the Arm by Nancy Farmer
    (Orchard/Richard Jackson)
1996
The Midwife's Apprentice by Karen Cushman
    (Clarion)
Honor Books
What Jamie Saw by Carolyn Coman (Front Street)
The Watsons Go to Birmingham—1963 by
    Christopher Paul Curtis (Delacorte)
Yolonda's Genius by Carol Fenner (McElderry/
    Simon & Schuster)
The Great Fire by Jim Murphy (Scholastic)
1997
The View from Saturday by E. L. Konigsburg (Jean
    Karl/Atheneum)
Honor Books
A Girl Named Disaster by Nancy Farmer (Richard
    Jackson/Orchard)
Moorchild by Elois McGraw (McElderry)

The Thief by Megan Whalen Turner (Greenwillow)
Belle Prater's Boy by Ruth White (Farrar)
1998
Out of the Dust by Karen Hesse (Scholastic)
Honor Books
Ella Enchanted by Gail Carson Levine
    (HarperCollins)
Lily's Crossing by Patricia Reilly Giff (Delacorte)
Wringer by Jerry Spinelli (HarperCollins)
1999
Holes by Louis Sachar (Frances Foster)
Honor Book
A Long Way from Chicago by Richard Peck (Dial)
2000
Bud, Not Buddy by Christopher Paul Curtis
    (Delacorte)
Honor Books
Getting Near to Baby by Audrey Couloumbis
    (Putnam)
Our Only May Amelia by Jennifer L. Holm
    (HarperCollins)
26 Fairmount Avenue by Tomie de Paola (Putnam)
2001
A Year Down Yonder by Richard Peck (Dial)
Honor Books
Hope Was Here by Joan Bauer (Putnam's)
Because of Winn-Dixie by Kate DiCamillo
    (Candlewick)
Joey Pigza Loses Control by Jack Gantos (Farrar,
    Straus, & Giroux)
The Wanderer by Sharon Creech (HarperCollins)

Randolph Caldecott Medal

The Randolph Caldecott Medal, named in honor of the nineteenth-century illustrator of children's books, is awarded annually under the supervision of the Association for Library Service to Children of the American Library Association. It is awarded to the illustrator of the most distinguished children's book published in the United States in the previous year. Usually, one or more Honor Books are also chosen. The award is limited to residents or citizens of the United States.

1938
Animals of the Bible by Helen Dean Fish, illustrated
    by Dorothy P. Lathrop (Lippincott)
Honor Books
Four and Twenty Blackbirds by Helen Dean Fish,
    illustrated by Robert Lawson (Stokes)
Seven Simeons by Boris Artzybasheff (Viking)
1939
Mei Li by Thomas Handforth (Doubleday)
Honor Books
Andy and the Lion by James Daugherty (Viking)
Barkis by Clare Newberry (Harper)
The Forest Pool by Laura Adams Armer (Longman)

Snow White and the Seven Dwarfs by Wanda Gág
    (Coward)
Wee Gillis by Munro Leaf, illustrated by Robert
    Lawson (Viking)
1940
Abraham Lincoln by Ingri and Edgar Parin
    D'Aulaire (Doubleday)
Honor Books
The Ageless Story by Lauren Ford (Dodd)
Cock-a-Doodle Doo by Berta and Elmer Hader
    (Macmillan)
Madeline by Ludwig Bemelmans
    (Viking)

1941
They Were Strong and Good by Robert Lawson (Viking)
Honor Book
April's Kittens by Clare Newberry (Harper)
1942
Make Way for Ducklings by Robert McCloskey
   (Viking)
Honor Books
An American ABC by Maud and Miska Petersham
   (Macmillan)
In My Mother's House by Ann Nolan Clark,
   illustrated by Velino Herrera (Viking)
Nothing at All by Wanda Gág (Coward)
Paddle-to-the-Sea by Holling C. Holling (Houghton
   Mifflin)
1943
The Little House by Virginia Lee Burton (Houghton
   Mifflin)
Honor Books
Dash and Dart by Mary and Conrad Buff (Viking)
Marshmallow by Clare Newberry (Harper)
1944
Many Moons by James Thurber, illustrated by
   Louis Slobodkin (Harcourt)
Honor Books
A Child's Good Night Book by Margaret Wise
   Brown, illustrated by Jean Charlot (Scott)
Good Luck Horse by Chin-Yi Chan, illustrated by
   Plao Chan (Whittlesey)
The Mighty Hunter by Berta and Elmer Hader
   (Macmillan)
Pierre Pigeon by Lee Kingman, illustrated by
   Arnold E. Bare (Houghton Mifflin)
Small Rain: Verses from the Bible selected by Jessie
   Orton Jones, illustrated by Elizabeth Orton
   Jones (Viking)
1945
Prayer for a Child by Rachel Field, illustrated by
   Elizabeth Orton Jones (Macmillan)
Honor Books
The Christmas Anna Angel by Ruth Sawyer,
   illustrated by Kate Seredy (Viking)
In the Forest by Marie Hall Ets (Viking)
Mother Goose illustrated by Tasha Tudor (Walck)
Yonie Wondernose by Marguerite de Angeli
   (Doubleday)
1946
The Rooster Crows (traditional Mother Goose)
   illustrated by Maud and Miska Petersham
   (Macmillan)
Honor Books
Little Lost Lamb by Golden MacDonald, illustrated
   by Leonard Weisgard (Doubleday)
*My Mother Is the Most Beautiful Woman in the
   World* by Becky Reyher, illustrated by Ruth C.
   Gannett (Lothrop)
Sing Mother Goose by Opal Wheeler, illustrated by
   Marjorie Torrey (Dutton)
You Can Write Chinese by Kurt Wiese (Viking)

1947
The Little Island by Golden MacDonald, illustrated
   by Leonard Weisgard (Doubleday)
Honor Books
Boats on the River by Marjorie Flack, illustrated by
   Jay Hyde Barnum (Viking)
Pedro, the Angel of Olvera Street by Leo Politi
   (Scribner's)
Rain Drop Splash by Alvin Tresselt, illustrated by
   Leonard Weisgard (Lothrop)
Sing in Praise: A Collection of the Best Loved Hymns
   by Opal Wheeler, illustrated by Marjorie
   Torrey (Dutton)
Timothy Turtle by Al Graham, illustrated by Tony
   Palazzo (Welch)
1948
White Snow, Bright Snow by Alvin Tresselt,
   illustrated by Roger Duvoisin (Lothrop)
Honor Books
Bambino the Clown by George Schreiber (Viking)
McElligot's Pool by Dr. Seuss (Random House)
Roger and the Fox by Lavinia Davis, illustrated by
   Hildegard Woodward (Doubleday)
Song of Robin Hood edited by Anne Malcolmson,
   illustrated by Virginia Lee Burton (Houghton
   Mifflin)
Stone Soup by Marcia Brown (Scribner's)
1949
The Big Snow by Berta and Elmer Hader
   (Macmillan)
Honor Books
All Around the Town by Phyllis McGinley,
   illustrated by Helen Stone (Lippincott)
Blueberries for Sal by Robert McCloskey (Viking)
Fish in the Air by Kurt Wiese (Viking)
Juanita by Leo Politi (Scribner's)
1950
Song of the Swallows by Leo Politi (Scribner's)
Honor Books
America's Ethan Allen by Stewart Holbrook,
   illustrated by Lynd Ward (Houghton Mifflin)
Bartholomew and the Oobleck by Dr. Seuss (Random
   House)
The Happy Day by Ruth Krauss, illustrated by
   Marc Simont (Harper)
Henry Fisherman by Marcia Brown (Scribner's)
The Wild Birthday Cake by Lavinia Davis, illus-
   trated by Hildegard Woodward (Doubleday)
1951
The Egg Tree by Katherine Milhous (Scribner's)
Honor Books
Dick Whittington and His Cat by Marcia Brown
   (Scribner's)
If I Ran the Zoo by Dr. Seuss (Random House)
The Most Wonderful Doll in the World by Phyllis
   McGinley, illustrated by Helen Stone
   (Lippincott)
T-Bone, the Baby Sitter by Clare Newberry (Harper)
The Two Reds by Will, illustrated by Nicolas
   (Harcourt)

1952
Finders Keepers by Will, illustrated by Nicolas (Harcourt)
Honor Books
All Falling Down by Gene Zion, illustrated by Margaret Bloy Graham (Harper)
Bear Party by William Pène du Bois (Viking)
Feather Mountain by Elizabeth Olds (Houghton Mifflin)
Mr. T. W. Anthony Woo by Marie Hall Ets (Viking)
Skipper John's Cook by Marcia Brown (Scribner's)

1953
The Biggest Bear by Lynd Ward (Houghton Mifflin)
Honor Books
Ape in a Cape by Fritz Eichenberg (Harcourt)
Five Little Monkeys by Juliet Kepes (Houghton Mifflin)
One Morning in Maine by Robert McCloskey (Viking)
Puss in Boots by Charles Perrault, illustrated by Marcia Brown (Scribner's)
The Storm Book by Charlotte Zolotow, illustrated by Margaret Bloy Graham (Harper)

1954
Madeline's Rescue by Ludwig Bemelmans (Viking)
Honor Books
A Very Special House by Ruth Krauss, illustrated by Maurice Sendak (Harper)
Green Eyes by A. Birnbaum (Capitol)
Journey Cake, Ho! by Ruth Sawyer, illustrated by Robert McCloskey (Viking)
The Steadfast Tin Soldier by Hans Christian Andersen, illustrated by Marcia Brown (Scribner's)
When Will the World Be Mine? by Miriam Schlein, illustrated by Jean Charlot (Scott)

1955
Cinderella, or the Little Glass Slipper by Charles Perrault, illustrated by Marcia Brown (Scribner's)
Honor Books
Book of Nursery and Mother Goose Rhymes, illustrated by Marguerite de Angeli (Doubleday)
The Thanksgiving Story by Alice Dalgliesh, illustrated by Helen Sewell (Scribner's)
Wheel on the Chimney by Margaret Wise Brown, illustrated by Tibor Gergely (Lippincott)

1956
Frog Went A-Courtin' retold by John Langstaff, illustrated by Feodor Rojankovsky (Harcourt)
Honor Books
Crow Boy by Taro Yashima (Viking)
Play with Me by Marie Hall Ets (Viking)

1957
A Tree Is Nice by Janice May Udry, illustrated by Marc Simont (Harper)
Honor Books
Anatole by Eve Titus, illustrated by Paul Galdone (McGraw-Hill)
Gillespie and the Guards by Benjamin Elkin, illustrated by James Daugherty (Viking)

Lion by William Pène du Bois (Viking)
Mr. Penny's Race Horse by Marie Hall Ets (Viking)
1 Is One by Tasha Tudor (Walck)

1958
Time of Wonder by Robert McCloskey (Viking)
Honor Books
Anatole and the Cat by Eve Titus, illustrated by Paul Galdone (McGraw-Hill)
Fly High, Fly Low by Don Freeman (Viking)

1959
Chanticleer and the Fox adapted from Chaucer, illustrated by Barbara Cooney (Crowell)
Honor Books
The House That Jack Built by Antonio Frasconi (Harcourt)
Umbrella by Taro Yashima (Viking)
What Do You Say, Dear? by Sesyle Joslin, illustrated by Maurice Sendak (Scott)

1960
Nine Days to Christmas by Marie Hall Ets and Aurora Labastida, illustrated by Marie Hall Ets (Viking)
Honor Books
Houses from the Sea by Alice E. Goudey, illustrated by Adrienne Adams (Scribner's)
The Moon Jumpers by Janice May Udry, illustrated by Maurice Sendak (Harper)

1961
Baboushka and the Three Kings by Ruth Robbins, illustrated by Nicholas Sidjakov (Parnassus)
Honor Book
Inch by Inch by Leo Lionni (Astor-Honor)

1962
Once a Mouse by Marcia Brown (Scribner's)
Honor Books
The Day We Saw the Sun Come Up by Alice E. Goudey, illustrated by Adrienne Adams (Scribner's)
The Fox Went Out on a Chilly Night, illustrated by Peter Spier (Doubleday)
Little Bear's Visit by Else Holmelund Minarik, illustrated by Maurice Sendak (Harper)

1963
The Snowy Day by Ezra Jack Keats (Viking)
Honor Books
Mr. Rabbit and the Lovely Present by Charlotte Zolotow, illustrated by Maurice Sendak (Harper)
The Sun Is a Golden Earring by Natalia M. Belting, illustrated by Bernarda Bryson (Holt)

1964
Where the Wild Things Are by Maurice Sendak (Harper)
Honor Books
All in the Morning Early by Sorche Nic Leodhas, illustrated by Evaline Ness (Holt)
Mother Goose and Nursery Rhymes, illustrated by Philip Reed (Atheneum)
Swimmy by Leo Lionni (Pantheon)

1965
May I Bring a Friend? by Beatrice Schenk
de Regniers, illustrated by Beni Montresor
(Atheneum)
Honor Books
A Pocketful of Cricket by Rebecca Caudill, illustrated
by Evaline Ness (Holt)
Rain Makes Applesauce by Julian Scheer, illustrated
by Marvin Bileck (Holiday House)
The Wave by Margaret Hodges, illustrated by Blair
Lent (Houghton Mifflin)
1966
Always Room for One More by Sorche Nic Leodhas,
illustrated by Nonny Hogrogian (Holt)
Honor Books
Hide and Seek Fog by Alvin Tresselt, illustrated by
Roger Duvoisin (Lothrop)
Just Me by Marie Hall Ets (Viking)
Tom Tit Tot by Evaline Ness (Scribner's)
1967
Sam, Bangs & Moonshine by Evaline Ness (Holt)
Honor Book
One Wide River to Cross by Barbara Emberley,
illustrated by Ed Emberley (Prentice-Hall)
1968
Drummer Hoff by Barbara Emberley, illustrated by
Ed Emberley (Prentice-Hall)
Honor Books
The Emperor and the Kite by Jane Yolen, illustrated
by Ed Young (World)
Frederick by Leo Lionni (Pantheon)
Seashore Story by Taro Yashima (Viking)
1969
The Fool of the World and the Flying Ship retold by
Arthur Ransome, illustrated by Uri Shulevitz
(Farrar)
Honor Book
Why the Sun and the Moon Live in the Sky by
Elphinstone Dayrell, illustrated by Blair Lent
(Houghton Mifflin)
1970
Sylvester and the Magic Pebble by William Steig
(Windmill/Simon & Schuster)
Honor Books
Alexander and the Wind-Up Mouse by Leo Lionni
(Pantheon)
Goggles! by Ezra Jack Keats (Macmillan)
The Judge by Harve Zemach, illustrated by Margot
Zemach (Farrar)
Pop Corn & Ma Goodness by Edna Mitchell
Preston,
illustrated by Robert Andrew Parker (Viking)
Thy Friend, Obadiah by Brinton Turkle (Viking)
1971
A Story, a Story by Gail E. Haley (Atheneum)
Honor Books
The Angry Moon by William Sleator, illustrated by
Blair Lent (Atlantic/Little, Brown)

Frog and Toad Are Friends by Arnold Lobel
(Harper)
In the Night Kitchen by Maurice Sendak (Harper)
1972
One Fine Day by Nonny Hogrogian (Macmillan)
Honor Books
Hildilid's Night by Cheli Durán Ryan, illustrated
by Arnold Lobel (Macmillan)
If All the Seas Were One Sea by Janina Domanska
(Macmillan)
Moja Means One by Muriel Feelings, illustrated
by Tom Feelings (Dial)
1973
The Funny Little Woman retold by Arlene Mosel,
illustrated by Blair Lent (Dutton)
Honor Books
Anansi the Spider adapted and illustrated by
Gerald McDermott (Holt)
Hosie's Alphabet by Hosea, Tobias, and Lisa
Baskin,
illustrated by Leonard Baskin (Viking)
Snow White and the Seven Dwarfs, illustrated by
Nancy Eckholm Burkert (Farrar)
When Clay Sings by Byrd Baylor, illustrated by
Tom Bahti (Scribner's)
1974
Duffy and the Devil retold by Harve Zemach,
illustrated by Margot Zemach (Farrar)
Honor Books
Cathedral by David Macaulay (Houghton Mifflin)
Three Jovial Huntsmen by Susan Jeffers (Bradbury)
1975
Arrow to the Sun by Gerald McDermott (Viking)
Honor Book
Jambo Means Hello by Muriel Feelings, illustrated
by Tom Feelings (Dial)
1976
Why Mosquitoes Buzz in People's Ears by Verna
Aardema, illustrated by Leo and Diane Dillon
(Dial)
Honor Books
The Desert Is Theirs by Byrd Baylor, illustrated by
Peter Parnall (Scribner's)
Strega Nona retold and illustrated by Tomie
de Paola (Prentice)
1977
Ashanti to Zulu: African Traditions by Margaret
Musgrove, illustrated by Leo and Diane Dillon
(Dial)
Honor Books
The Amazing Bone by William Steig (Farrar)
The Contest retold and illustrated by Nonny
Hogrogian (Greenwillow)
Fish for Supper by M. B. Goffstein (Dial)
The Golem by Beverly Brodsky McDermott
(Lippincott)
Hawk, I'm Your Brother by Byrd Baylor, illustrated
by Peter Parnall (Scribner's)

1978
Noah's Ark illustrated by Peter Spier (Doubleday)
Honor Books
Castle by David Macaulay (Houghton Mifflin)
It Could Always Be Worse by Margot Zemach
  (Farrar)
1979
The Girl Who Loved Wild Horses by Paul Goble
  (Bradbury)
Honor Books
Freight Train by Donald Crews (Greenwillow)
The Way to Start a Day by Byrd Baylor, illustrated
  by Peter Parnall (Scribner's)
1980
Ox-Cart Man by Donald Hall, illustrated by
  Barbara Cooney (Viking)
Honor Books
Ben's Trumpet by Rachel Isadora (Greenwillow)
The Garden of Abdul Gasazi by Chris Van Allsburg
  (Houghton Mifflin)
The Treasure by Uri Shulevitz (Farrar)
1981
Fables by Arnold Lobel (Harper)
Honor Books
The Bremen Town Musicians retold and illustrated
  by Ilse Plume (Doubleday)
The Grey Lady and the Strawberry Snatcher by Molly
  Bang (Four Winds)
Mice Twice by Joseph Low (McElderry)
Truck by Donald Crews (Greenwillow)
1982
Jumanji by Chris Van Allsburg (Houghton Mifflin)
Honor Books
On Market Street by Arnold Lobel, illustrated by
  Anita Lobel (Greenwillow)
Outside Over There by Maurice Sendak (Harper)
*A Visit to William Blake's Inn: Poems for Innocent
  and Experienced Travelers* by Nancy Willard,
  illustrated by Alice and Martin Provensen
  (Harcourt)
Where the Buffaloes Begin by Olaf Baker, illustrated
  by Stephen Gammell (Warne)
1983
Shadow by Blaise Cendrars, illustrated by Marcia
  Brown (Scribner's)
Honor Books
A Chair for My Mother by Vera B. Williams
  (Greenwillow)
When I Was Young in the Mountains by Cynthia
  Rylant, illustrated by Diane Goode (Dutton)
1984
*The Glorious Flight: Across the Channel with Louis
  Blériot* by Alice and Martin Provensen (Viking)
Honor Books
Little Red Riding Hood retold and illustrated by
  Trina Schart Hyman (Holiday House)
Ten, Nine, Eight by Molly Bang (Greenwillow)

1985
Saint George and the Dragon by Margaret Hodges,
  illustrated by Trina Schart Hyman (Little,
  Brown)
Honor Books
Hansel and Gretel retold by Rika Lesser, illustrated
  by Paul O. Zelinsky (Dodd)
Have You Seen My Duckling? by Nancy Tafuri
  (Greenwillow)
The Story of Jumping Mouse retold and illustrated
  by John Steptoe (Lothrop)
1986
The Polar Express by Chris Van Allsburg
  (Houghton Mifflin)
Honor Books
King Bidgood's in the Bathtub by Audrey Wood,
  illustrated by Don Wood (Harcourt)
The Relatives Came by Cynthia Rylant, illustrated
  by Stephen Gammell (Bradbury)
1987
Hey, Al by Arthur Yorinks, illustrated by Richard
  Egielski (Farrar)
Honor Books
Alphabatics by Suse MacDonald (Bradbury)
Rumpelstiltskin by Paul O. Zelinsky (Dutton)
The Village of Round and Square Houses by Ann
  Grifalconi (Little, Brown)
1988
Owl Moon by Jane Yolen, illustrated by John
  Schoenherr (Philomel)
Honor Book
Mufaro's Beautiful Daughters: An African Tale by
  John Steptoe (Lothrop)
1989
Song and Dance Man by Karen Ackerman,
  illustrated by Stephen Gammell (Knopf)
Honor Books
The Boy of the Three-Year Nap by Dianne Snyder,
  illustrated by Allen Say (Houghton Mifflin)
Free-Fall by David Wiesner (Lothrop)
Goldilocks and the Three Bears by James Marshall (Dial)
Mirandy and Brother Wind by Patricia C.
  McKissack, illustrated by Jerry Pinkney
  (Knopf)
1990
Lon Po Po: A Red-Riding Hood Story from China
  translated and illustrated by Ed Young
  (Philomel)
Honor Books
Bill Peet: An Autobiography by Bill Peet (Houghton
  Mifflin)
Color Zoo by Lois Ehlert (Lippincott)
Hershel and the Hanukkah Goblins by Eric Kimmel,
  illustrated by Trina Schart Hyman (Holiday
  House)
The Talking Eggs by Robert D. San Souci,
  illustrated by Jerry Pinkney (Dial)

1991

Black and White by David Macaulay (Houghton Mifflin)

Honor Books

"More More More," Said the Baby: 3 Love Stories by Vera B. Williams (Greenwillow)

Puss in Boots by Charles Perrault, translated by Malcolm Arthur, illustrated by Fred Marcellino (Farrar)

1992

Tuesday by David Wiesner (Clarion)

Honor Book

Tar Beach by Faith Ringgold (Crown)

1993

Mirette on the High Wire by Emily Arnold McCully (Putnam)

Honor Books

Seven Blind Mice by Ed Young (Philomel)

The Stinky Cheese Man and Other Fairly Stupid Tales by Jon Scieszka, illustrated by Lane Smith (Viking)

Working Cotton by Sherley Anne Williams, illustrated by Carole Byard (Harcourt)

1994

Grandfather's Journey by Allen Say (Houghton Mifflin)

Honor Books

Owen by Kevin Henkes (Greenwillow)

Peppe, the Lamplighter by Elisa Bartone (Lothrop)

Raven by Gerald McDermott (Harcourt)

In the Small, Small Pond by Denise Fleming (Holt)

Yo! Yes? by Chris Raschka (Orchard)

1995

Smoky Night by Eve Bunting, illustrated by David Diaz (Harcourt)

Honor Books

Swamp Angel by Anne Isaacs, illustrated by Paul O. Zelinsky (Dutton)

John Henry by Julius Lester, illustrated by Jerry Pinkney (Dial)

Time Flies by Eric Rohmann (Crown)

1996

Officer Buckle and Gloria by Peggy Rathmann (Putnam)

Honor Books

Alphabet City by Stephen T. Johnson (Viking)

Zin! Zin! Zin! A Violin by Lloyd Moss (Simon & Schuster)

The Faithful Friend by Robert D. San Souci, illustrated by Brian Pinkney (Simon & Schuster)

Tops & Bottoms adapted and illustrated by Janet Stevens (Harcourt)

1997

Golem by David Wisniewski (Clarion)

Honor Books

Hush! A Thai Lullaby by Minfong Ho, illustrated by Holly Meade (Kroupa/Orchard)

The Graphic Alphabet by Neal Porter, illustrated by David Pelletier (Orchard)

The Paperboy by Dav Pilkey (Jackson/Orchard)

Starry Messenger by Peter Sis (Foster/Farrar)

1998

Rapunzel retold and illustrated by Paul O. Zelinsky (Dutton)

Honor Books

The Garden by Sarah Stewart, illustrated by David Small (Farrar)

Harlem by Walter Dean Myers, illustrated by Christopher Myers (Scholastic)

There Was an Old Lady Who Swallowed a Fly by Sims Taback (Viking)

1999

Snowflake Bentley by Jacqueline Briggs Martin, illustrated by Mary Azarian (Houghton Mifflin)

Honor Books

Duke Ellington: The Piano Prince and the Orchestra by Andrea Davis Pinkney, illustrated by Brian Pinkney (Hyperion)

No, David! by David Shannon (Scholastic)

Snow by Uri Shulevitz (Farrar, Straus, & Giroux)

Tibet through the Red Box by Peter Sis (Frances Foster)

2000

Joseph Had a Little Overcoat by Simms Taback (Viking)

Honor Books

A Child's Calendar by John Updike, illustrated by Trina Schart Hyman (Holiday House)

Sector 7 by David Wiesner (Clarion)

When Sophie Gets Angry—Really, Really Angry by Molly Bang (Scholastic)

The Ugly Duckling by Hans Christian Andersen, adapted and illustrated by Jerry Pinkney (Morrow)

2001

So You Want to Be President? by Judith St. George, illustrated by David Small (Philomel)

Honor Books

Casey at the Bat: A Ballad of the Republic Sung in the Year 1888 by Ernest Lawrence Thayer, illustrated by Christopher Bing (Handprint)

Click, Clack, Moo: Cows That Type by Doreen Cronin, illustrated by Betsy Lewin (Simon & Schuster

Olivia by Ian Falconer (Atheneum)